Street by Street

NORTHAMPTON
WELLINGBOROUGH
HIGHAM FERRERS, IRTHLINGBOROUGH, RAUNDS, RUSHDEN

Althorp Park, Blisworth, Brixworth, Bugbrooke, Earls Barton, Finedon, Irchester, Moulton, Pitsford, Roade, Stanwick, Sywell, Wollaston, Wootton

2nd edition March 2006
© Automobile Association Developments Limited 2006

Original edition printed July 2003

Ordnance Survey® This product includes map data licensed from Ordnance Survey® with the permission of the Controller of Her Majesty's Stationery Office. © Crown copyright 2006. All rights reserved. Licence number 399221.

Published by AA Publishing (a trading name of Automobile Association Developments Limited, whose registered office is Fanum House, Basing View, Basingstoke, Hampshire RG21 4EA. Registered number 1878835).

Mapping produced by the Cartography Department of The Automobile Association. (A02655)

A CIP Catalogue record for this book is available from the British Library.

Printed by Oriental Press in Dubai

The contents of this atlas are believed to be correct at the time of the latest revision. However, the publishers cannot be held responsible or liable for any loss or damage occasioned to any person acting or refraining from action as a result of any use or reliance on any material in this atlas, nor for any errors, omissions or changes in such material. This does not affect your statutory rights. The publishers would welcome information to correct any errors or omissions and to keep this atlas up to date. Please write to Publishing, The Automobile Association, Fanum House (FH12), Basing View, Basingstoke, Hampshire, RG21 4EA.

Ref: ML144z

Key to map pages	ii-iii
Key to map symbols	iv-1
Enlarged map pages	2-3
Main map pages	4-73
Index – towns & villages	74
Index – streets	74-82
Index – featured places	82-83
Acknowledgements	83

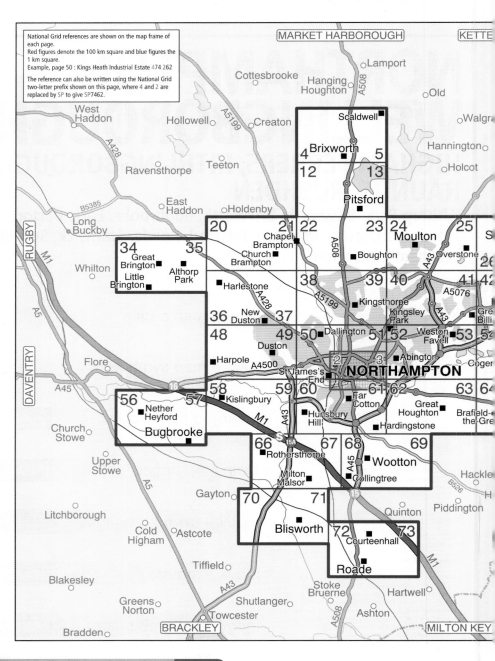

National Grid references are shown on the map frame of each page.
Red figures denote the 100 km square and blue figures the 1 km square.
Example, page 50 : Kings Heath Industrial Estate 474 262

The reference can also be written using the National Grid two-letter prefix shown on this page, where 4 and 2 are replaced by SP to give SP7462.

MARKET HARBOROUGH

KETTE

Lamport

Cottesbrooke

Hanging Houghton

Old

West Haddon

Hollowell

Creaton

Scaldwell

Walgra

Brixworth

Hannington

Holcot

Ravensthorpe

Teeton

4

5

12

13

Pitsford

East Haddon

Holdenby

Long Buckby

20

21

22

23

24

25

S

Moulton

Great Brington

34

35

Chapel Brampton

Church Brampton

Boughton

Overstone

Whilton

Little Brington

Althorp Park

Harlestone

38

39

40

41

42

Kingsthorpe

Kingsley Park

Gre Billi

36

37

New Duston

Dallington

51

52

Weston Favell

53

5

48

49

50

Duston

2

3

Abington

Coger

Harpole

St James's End

NORTHAMPTON

Flore

56

57

58

Kislingbury

59

60

Far Cotton

61

62

63

64

Nether Heyford

Hunsbury Hill

Great Houghton

Brafield-the Gre

Church Stowe

Bugbrooke

66

Rothersthorpe

67

68

69

Hardingstone

Wootton

Hackle

Upper Stowe

Milton Malsor

Collingtree

Gayton

70

71

Quinton

Piddington

Litchborough

Blisworth

72

73

Cold Higham

Astcote

Courteenhall

Tiffield

Roade

H

Blakesley

Stoke Bruerne

Hartwell

Greens Norton

Shutlanger

Ashton

Towcester

Bradden

BRACKLEY

MILTON KEY

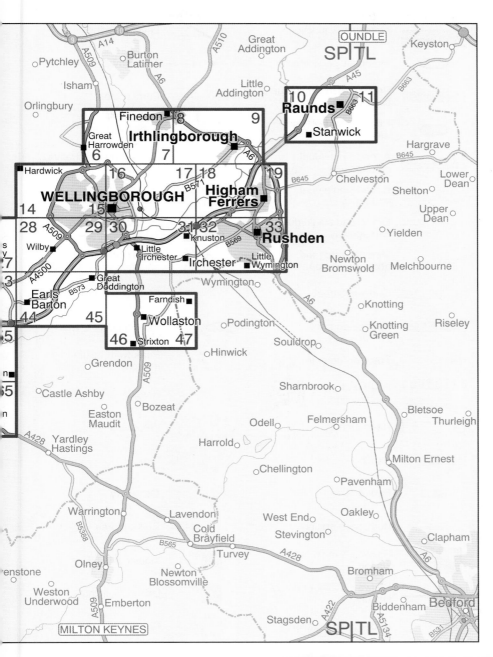

iv

Junction 9	Motorway & junction	*LC*	Level crossing
Services	Motorway service area	•—•—•—•	Tramway
	Primary road single/dual carriageway	-----------	Ferry route
Services	Primary road service area	....	Airport runway
	A road single/dual carriageway	– · – · – · –	County, administrative boundary
	B road single/dual carriageway	▼▼▼▼▼▼▼▼	Mounds
	Other road single/dual carriageway	**17**	Page continuation 1:15,000
	Minor/private road, access may be restricted	**3**	Page continuation to enlarged scale 1:10,000
← ←	One-way street		River/canal, lake, pier
	Pedestrian area		Aqueduct, lock, weir
------------	Track or footpath	465 ▲ Winter Hill	Peak (with height in metres)
	Road under construction		Beach
⌐ - - - - ⌐	Road tunnel		Woodland
P	Parking		Park
P+	Park & Ride	† † † † †	Cemetery
🚌	Bus/coach station		Built-up area
	Railway & main railway station		Industrial building
	Railway & minor railway station		Leisure building
⊖	Underground station		Retail building
⊖	Light railway & station		Other building
+++++++++	Preserved private railway		

⚞⚟⚞⚟	City wall	♜	Castle
A&E	Hospital with 24-hour A&E department	🏛	Historic house or building
PO	Post Office	Wakehurst Place NT	National Trust property
📖	Public library	Ⓜ	Museum or art gallery
ℹ	Tourist Information Centre	♞	Roman antiquity
ℹ	Seasonal Tourist Information Centre	⚱	Ancient site, battlefield or monument
⛽⛽	Petrol station, 24 hour Major suppliers only	🏭	Industrial interest
†	Church/chapel	❁	Garden
🚻	Public toilets	◉	Garden Centre Garden Centre Association Member
♿	Toilet with disabled facilities	🌳	Garden Centre Wyevale Garden Centre
PH	Public house AA recommended	🌲	Arboretum
🍴	Restaurant AA inspected	🛒	Farm or animal centre
Madeira Hotel	Hotel AA inspected	🦌	Zoological or wildlife collection
🎭	Theatre or performing arts centre	🦜	Bird collection
👥	Cinema	🐋	Nature reserve
⚑	Golf course	🐠	Aquarium
▲	Camping AA inspected	Ⓥ	Visitor or heritage centre
🚐	Caravan site AA inspected	♔	Country park
▲🚐	Camping & caravan site AA inspected	◉	Cave
🎡	Theme park	✖	Windmill
🏰	Abbey, cathedral or priory	🛢	Distillery, brewery or vineyard

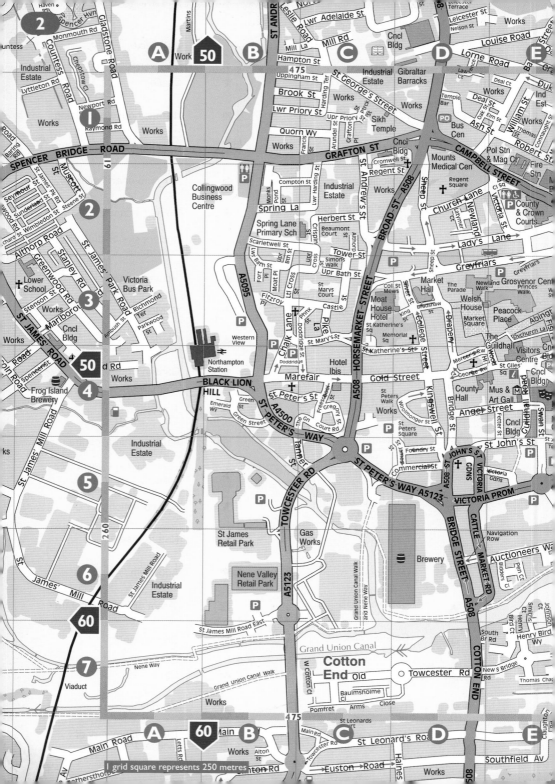

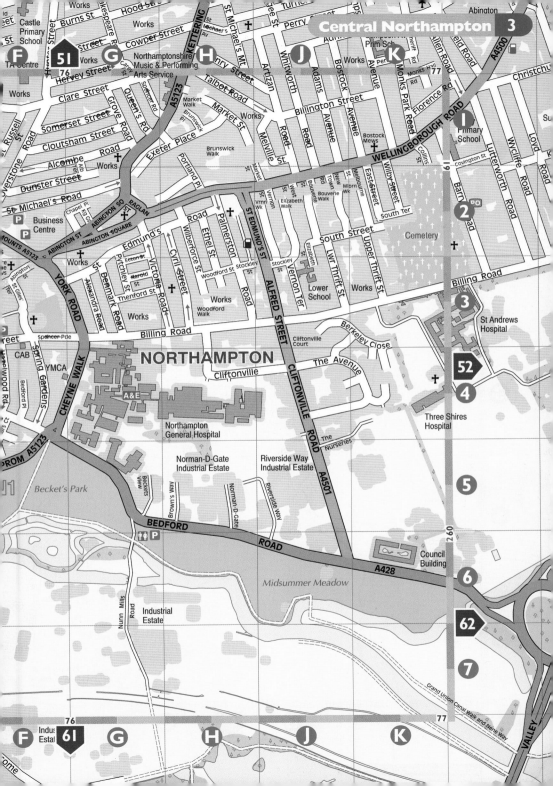

E
F
Lodge
Farm
76
G
H
School Lane
West
End
77
East End
Peters
Lane
Back
Lane
Holcot Lane
1

Scaldwell

HARBOROUGH ROAD

A508

Scaldwell Road

72

Rectory
Farm
2

3

Morgan Dr

Inner Av

Scaldwell Road

71

Quarry Rd

Laundon's
Lodge

4

Holcot Road

Holcot Road

ree Way

Burrows Vale
Waterpike
Hen Cl
The Ridings
Grass
Slade Dmsw
reach
Borough
The Ashway
The Knoll
Wheeldon Rd
iron
phimet
The Ashway
Wtrn Hng
Jnpr Jnpr
Knightons Wy
iridgew Wy

A508

Grange
Farm
5

270

E
F
13
76
G
H
77

Westfield Lodge

Cemetery

Station Rd

Tainty Cl

Tingdene Rd
Albert Rd
Victoria Rd
Orchard Cl

Tann Road

Rose Hill

Works

Hyde Drive
Rockleigh
Almarton

Rock Rd

Orchard Road

Finedon Infant Sch

High Street

Avenue Road
Berry Gn Rd

Well Street

Obelisk Rd

Finedon Mulso
CE Jnr Sch

Mulso Rd
A6
Hawthorne Rd

Mackworth Dr

Holly Wk

Church Hl
Stocks Hl

Church Street

Regent Street

Affleck
Pembridge

The Summerlee
Medical Centre

Works

Finedon

Dolben Cl

Bell Hill

Ivy Lane

Laws La
Ivy La

PO

Milner Road

Cromer Road

Ewenfield Road

Kenmuir Road

Hall Drive

Grove Way

A510

WELLINGBOROUGH ROAD

Harrowden Road

Hillside Farm

RYEBURY HILL

3

8

4

5

Finedon Road
Industrial Estate

Sidegate Works

Sidegate Lane

Carrol Spring Farm

WELLINGBOROUGH RD

I 7

Ise Valley

Finedonhill

New Barn
Farm

Raunds Town
FC

E
F
G
N
Farm
H

BRICK KILN ROAD
500
01

Crispin Way St
Nichols Wy
Orwell Cl
Nene Cl
Enterprise Rd
BRICK KILN ROAD

Mallows Drive
Wm Cl
McInnes Way
North St
HIGH ST

I

Webb Road
Windmill
De Ferneus Dr
Fmlsc Rd
T B C
73

Cemetery
York Wy
Ellison
Bugby Wy
Rotton Row
Church St
Burystead
MIDLAND ROAD
Brooks
Farm

Fairoaks Drive
Lane
HS Cl
E L Rd
St
Heritage Wy
Brooks Road

Ramsay
Whitefield
Gardner
Oakleigh
Langham Road
Lee St
Ch Vw
Berris
Der Pl
Richardson
Way

Twyford Av
Welbourne
Cl
Poplars
Miller St
W Gv
Manor St
Ponds Cl
Works
Butts
Derling Dr
Holmfield
Dr
Kingsmith

Windmill
Primary
School
M Cl
Windmill Av
The Sq
Spencer
St
Mnr Farm Rd
Broadlands
Viceroy Cl
Roman Wy
Saxon
Wy

Marshall's
The
Delves
Coggins
Cl
Ashfield
Road
Spinney St
Hill
Street
B663
BROOK STREET
Hollgton
Lawson St
Park Street
Mountbatten Way
Mountbatten Wy
B663
STATION

RAUNDS
Grombold
Ashfield Avenue
PO
Clmn St
Clare St
Harcourt St
Park
Infant
School
St Peters
CE Junior
School
Manor
Farm

Belmont
Gdns
Works
Thorpe St
Primrose
Gdns
Park Av

Dryden St
Mackenzie Road
GROVE ST
Sheffield
Ct
Warwick
Cl
Newtown Rd
Holmes Av
Rands Wy

Titty Ho
WELLINGTON ROAD
Chmbrln
Wy
Shortwoods
Cl
Newtown Road

Darsdale
Farm

B663

Shelton Road

500
01

E
F
G
H

73
2
72
3
4
5
271

Grange
Farm

E   F   **5**   G   H

76   77   70

I

Brixworth
Country Park

Pitsford Reservoir

2

Moulton
Grange
Farm

69

Moulton
Grange

Grange   Lane

3

Works   Works

Works

Lane

NN6

Grange

4

Springhill
Farm   The
Dovecote

Church La   Manor Rd

Glebe La   Pitsford   Broadlands
Primary Sch

268

Pitsford

Drummond Close   The Chase

PO   High   Street

5

Northamptonshire
Grammar School   Stable Ct

76   77

E   F   **23**   G   H

Home
Farm

Moulton

Stud
Farm

E F G 6 H

A509

A510 NORTHEN WAY

Goodwin

88 89 70

Grange Road

Holme Cl
The Meadows
Gilley
Appleby Cl
The Farm
The Pastures
Oak Vw
Y

Redhill
Fallowfield
Fallowfield
Fallowfield
The Banks

PO Farm Rd

A510

Wilkie Road
Aiken Cl

Calvert
Hunt Cl
Cooper Drive

I

Nest
Nest

WAY

Haddon Cl

A5193

Ashton Gv
Barnwell Road
Ashby
Ashby Road

Chatsworth Drive
Hatfield Close
Chepstow Drive
Mulfield
Wentworth
Avenue
Gleneagles
Littledale

Orton
Althorp
Lowick
Barnwell
Brampt
Naseby Cl

Redwell
Leisure
Centre

Redwell
Infant Sch

Crawley Av Churchill Av
Blenheim Rd
Sparke Cl
Westminster
Hulme
Tudor Wy
Kilborn Road

Varley Cl
Piper Cl
Constable Dr
Turner Cl
Lowry
Reynolds
Kilborn Cl

Med Cen

Spencelayh
Close
Leighton

Oakway
Pearmain Av
Cedar
Ridgeway

Plumtree Av
Cherry
A509

Oakway
Junior
School

HARROWDEN

Sir Christopher
on School

Merford Road
Vicarage
Torrington Road
Devonshire
Close

Wellingborough
Town CC

Weir Cl
Roche Wy
The Headlands
Sandy Cl

The Pightle

16

Hardwick Road
Kendal
Windermere
Penrith Dr
Hardwick Road
Hardwick Road

**Hatton
Park**

Redwell Rd
Whytewell Rd
Works

Gold Street
The Avenue
Med Cen
Works
Inf Sch

Coniston
Inf Sch
Med Cen

Olympic Way
Minerva Way

Queensway
Kilnway

Hardwick County
Junior School

Laburnham
Close
Severn
Close
Maple Drive
Bush Close
Mulberry
Claydon Cl

Dybdale
Hardwick
Ryeburn Wy

Promenade
Hatton Park Road
Hatton Street
Debdale Rd
Works

Elm St
North Rd
Knights Ct
Outlaw Ln

George St
Havelock St
Herberts La

Inf Sch
Alliance Ter

4

Harrison
Close
Steele Road
Brickhill Road
Edwards Dr

Stream Bank
Close

Weavers
School

Jun
Sch

High
St

St John's St
Rock St
Buckwell End
Jacksons La

HIGH STREET
Med
Cen
Sch
Herberts La

CHURCH STREET

Ruskin Avenue
Masefield Road
Cowper Rd
Byron Rd
Keats Rd
Chaucer Rd

Weavers Road
Birchfield Rd
Ashfield Road
Roberts Street
Westfield
College St
Grove St
Arthur St

St Barnabas
CE School

County
Court
Cncl
Bldg
Works
West Villa Road
West Street

Cncl
Bldg

SILVER ST
The
Hind H

5

Cncl
Bldg

Friars
School

E F 29 G H

NORTHAMPTON ROAD

88

Oakley
Oakley Dr
Tennyson Rd
Fourth Av
Third Avenue
Western Way
Queensway
Clare Rd

Gillitts Road

Croyland Primary
School

Croyland
Road

OXFORD STREET
CROYLAND ROAD

Wood Street
Spring Gdns
Hill Street
Dale St
Abbots Way

89
Monks Way
B571

Wellingborough
Swimming Baths

E

Sidegate Lane

Carrol Spring Farm

F

92

G

8

H

93

70

West Field Lodge

1

WELLINGBO

Finedonhill Farm

Sidegate Lane

Stone Cross Farm

2

MILL ROAD

B571

69

Ditchford Road

3

18

South Hill Farm

IRTHLINGBOROUGH ROAD

South View Farm

Irthlingborough Grange

Works

4

268

5

E

F

92

31

Nene Way

G

93

H

20

Holdenby House
Falconry Centre

Holdenby

469   70

Holdenby
South Lodge

Glebe
Farm

A428

Glebe   Lane

35

36

Lower
Harlestone

Lane

I grid square represents 500 metres

22

Merry Tom Lane

A · B · 12 · C · D

4 73 74 80A

I

67

Spinney Farm

Pitsford Lodge Farm

Brampton Lane

Sedgebrook Hall

2

A5199

Cedar Hythe

Beck Lane

Close

oad

Pitsford & Brampton Station

Northampton & Lamport Railway

Sedgebrook Lodge

3

Pitsford Road

Brampton ary School

21

69

NORTHAMPTON ROAD

Boughton Grange

4

Brampton Grange

Boughton Mill Farm

rthamptonshire unty Golf Club

Glebe Farm

5

Golf Course

Brampton Lane

Westview Farm

2 65

4 73 74

White Hills

A · B · 38 · C · D

HARBOROUGH ROAD NORTH

White Hills Way

Central A

Fall Mile

Fallow Wk

PO

Grnhills Ct

Sandhills Rd

White Hills

The

Whitehills

High Stree

Northamptonshire Grammar School

Stable Ct

E   **F**   **13**   **G**   **H**

76   77

Home Farm

Stud Farm

I

Moulton Road

Pitsford Road

Fox Covert Hall

2

Bunkers Hill Farm

3

24

Butcher's Lane

Spectacle Lane

Boughton

Butcher's La

Spring Cl

Holly Lodge

4

Church St

Boughton Primary School

Vyse Road

Humfrey Lane

Moulton   Lane

Greville Cl

Boughton Green

Lower Farm Road

Howard Lane

Obelisk

Devonshire Cl

Green Road

Industrial Estate

5

Spinney Cl

Boughton

Tenter   Road

Tiverton

Obelisk Rise

Duncan Cl

RED   HOUSE   ROAD

Ash Rise

Obelisk Rise

Kings Park R

Summerhouse Road

Magistrates Court

E   **F**   **39**   **G**   **H**

76   77

St John's Av

Rev   Hnts

Way

Dixon

Moulton Business Park

Moulton Park

Sunnyside Lower School

All Saints CE VA Primary School

Regal Cl

Kyoto Cl

Deer

Holly Ldg

St John's Av

E F G H

84 85

The Grange

I

67

Highfield Road

Glebe Road

Mears Ashby Endowed Primary School

North Street

Mears Ashby

Nursery Ct

Tinkers Crs

Church Street

Bakehouse

Wellingborough Road

Vicarage La

2

Earls Barton Road

Manor Road

Lady's Lane

Paddock

Duchess End

Sywell Road

Wilby Road

Hill Farm

3

NN6

28

66

4

5

well Reservoir

265

Sywell Country Park

P

V

Washbrook Lane

Mears

84 85

E F G H

43

Ashby Road

White House Industrial Estate

Main Farm

MAIN ROAD

28

A   B   **14**   C   D

485   86

I

67

2

3

27

66

Mears Ashby Road

PARK FARM WAY

Wilby

Wilby CE
Primary
School

Church

Huxley Cl
Huxley
Cl

Park F
Industri
Estate

Napier Cl
Wallis Cl

Swinbur

Bu
Lor
Bo

Wordsworth Road

She

4

5

265

485   86   44   C   D

A   B

M   Road
Farm

Doddington Road

White House
Industrial Estate

ROAD

Wellingboro

Cemetery

I grid square represents 500 metres

I grid square represents 500 metres

E F **17** G H

92 93

I

67

Spinney

Nene Way

Knuston
Lodge Farm

2

Chester
House

Town
End
Farm

Chester   Road

3

Prologis
Park

Lower
Farm

32

66

HIGHAM ROAD A45

Nene Way

Barringers
Gdns

Cemetery

High   Street

Industrial
Estate

St
Kthrn's
Wy

NN29

Irchester
Country Park

School
Rd

School
Hl

Townwell
La

P

Irchester Community
Primary School

School
La

Health Cen

C H

4

LANE

Bakers
Crs

Bakers Crs

Wntg
Pl

Wantage Rd

New
St

Parsons Rd

Denton
Cl

Norman
Wy

B570

PO

HIGH
ST

East St

Manor
Cl

Saxon Ri

Austin

Bradshaw
Wy

Alfred St

WOLLASTON   ROAD

Gray St

Thrift St

Orchard

Ash Cl

Oak

London
Rd

Edward   End

Chpmns Rd

Arkwright   Road

Grn Cl

Warren Cl

Evelyn
Wy

Prospect Av

Berrill St

Road

James St

Rmn Wy

5

Beech

Larch

Rd
Cl

Pine

Cl

Pt Cl

Coulon
Cl

Woodlands

Farndish   Road

Irchester

265

92 93

E F G H

Irchester
Grange

34

A 465 B 66 C D

1

Moor Farm

Glebe Farm

2

Whilton Rd

Back La

Main Street

Great Bringt

PO PH

Back Lane

3

Hamilton Lane

4

Brington Primary School

5

Folly Lane

Blacksmithy's Lane

PH

Main Street

Hall Lane

Pine Ct

Steeple Lane

Little Brington

Church Farm

Macmillans W

A 465 B 66 C D

Hillcrest Cottage

2 64

1 grid square represents 500 metres

Works

E   F   G   H

68   69   66

Macmillans Way

I

20

NN7

2

Sir John's Wood

Althorp

Dog Pond

Althorp Park

65

3

Oaktree Stew

Chinkwell Spinney

Great Stew

Garden Stew

4

Harleston Forest

264   36

Yew Tree Farm

Harle

5

E   F   G   H

68   69

M...res Way

E   F   G   H

92   93

64

Farndish
✝

1

Grange
Farm

Irchester R

B569

IRCHESTER ROAD

Irchester Road

Irchester Road

Manor
Farm

2

Rectory
Farm

63

Tower
Farm

Francis Dickins
Close

Wollaston
School

Works

Wollaston

Northamptonshire County

Bedfordshire County

3

Hookhams

The Cap

T HS

Windmill Cl

Park Street

Poplar Pl

Path

Hinwick Road

Hinwick Road

William's

Raymond's

WV

Industrial
Estate

Lovett's
Farm

4

Hin

Shepherds

262

Hill

Lodge
Farm

5

H

The Sla

92   93

E   F   G   H

Poplars Farm

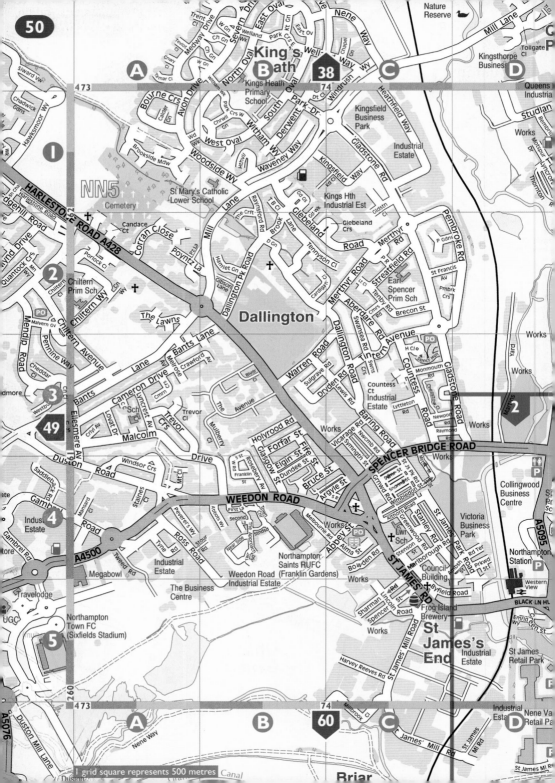

E F **43** G A45 H

84 85

Grendon

Nene Way

I

62

2

3

Nene Way

Mill Lane

Whiston Road

19

Roe
Farm

Whist n

4

Street

Manor Farm
Court

Place
House

†

Short La

The Firs

5

260

E F **65** G H

84 85

M1

A

B Heyford Mill

Dovecote Farm

C

MAIN ROAD

D

Upper Heyford

Hipwells

Midshires Way

465

66

1

Whitehall Farm

59

2

Church Lane

Manor Park

Weedon Rd

Cemy

Church Street

Middle Street

Watery La

arksd

PH

PO

The Bliss Charity School

Wakefield Way

Tanborough

3

The Pound

Winston Cl

Western Avenue

Rolfe Cres

Close Rd

Hillside Rd

Hillside Cres

Bugbrooke Rd

Nether Heyford

Works

58

Furnace Lane

South View

Heyford Wharf

4

Works

Grand Union Canal

Midshires Way

Midshires Way

Heyford Grange

New Creation Farm

5

257

Shallon Farm

465

66

A

B

C

D

257

Junction 16

Red Lion

E   F   G   Harper Mill   H

68   69

Nene Way

I

Bugbrooke Mill

59

M1

Nene Way

2

58

3

Johns Road

58

4

Manor Farm

Kislingbury Road

Corporation Farm

Campion School

Chipsey Av

Butts Hl Cl

Smitherway

Bugbrooke Primary School

Johns Road

Levitts Road

Shepherds Walk

Surgery

Beech Cl

Oaklands

Lime Cl

Almd Cl

Waggoners Wy

Homestead Dr

The Anvil

Church Lane

Badgers Cl

Maple Cl

Meadway

Ash Gv

Georges Avenue

5

The Paddocks

PO

Ace La

High Street

Harrison Ct

Moores Cl

Georges Cl

Bugbrooke

Great Lane

Browns Yard

Pilgrims Lane

Bugbrooke RUFC

The Ashes

West End

Peace Hl

The Leys

Pond La

Bugbrooke Sports & Community Centre

Camp Hill

Tibbitts La Wy

Midshires Way

E   F   G   H

68   69   2 57

E F **53** G H

80 81 60

Meadow Lane

Nursery Close

Grange Farm

Station Road

Little Houghton

I

Bedford Road

PO

Lodge Road

Home Acre

Bedford Road

Bedford Road

Lodge Cl

Little Houghton CE Primary School

A428

2

Cemetery

High Street

The Cross

Cherry Tree La

Willow Lane

Little La

The Hill

Dobson Close

Crackness La

Glebe La

Willow Crescent

Atterbury Wy

59

Lodge Road

3

64

Paget Close

The Green

Wy

Marsley

Cl

Farm Wy

Lime

Keats Cl

Leys Lane

Little Houghton Lodge

4

258

5

80 81

E F G H

Great Houghton Lodge Farm

E   F   55   G   H
84   85

I

2   Chad
     Lodge

59

3

Chadstone

Whiston Road

Castle
Ashby Lodge

4

258

Leys
Close
Dovecote Dr
Grange
Close
The Leys
Fishpond
Ct
Main Street
Church Wy
Denton
Orchard La
Surg
Vicarage Lane
Northampton Road
The La
Bedford
Meadow
Windmill Lane
Denton
Primary School
Cem
Br
Road
Wareing
Lane
By Pass
Way

5

Grange Farm

A428

E   F   G   H
84   85

Denton Road

A

B

59
72

C

Brook
Farm

D

471

1

Kislingbury Road

57

Grafton
Wy

Ardens
Gv

Mumford
Dr

St Johns
Close

Junc

Rothersthorpe Service Area

North Street

Banbury Lane

Rothersthorpe
CE Primary
School

Cem

Berry Cl

2

Church Street

The Lane

Rothersthorpe

56

Grand Union Canal

Grand Union Canal Walk

3

NN7

4

A43

5

255

471

A

Milton Road

B

70
72

Station
Rd

C

D

Landimore Road

E F 62 G H

78 79

I

Hardingstone
Lodge

Saucebridge
Farm

57

Pagnell
Court

B526

RD

Bush

rook Cl

Lordswood Cl
Ensfild Cl

Mal Greeve
High Greeve
Middle Greeve
Low Greeve
Greeve Wy

Lady Hollow Drive

Whittles Cross
Wickett Cl
Park Dene
Thrupp Br
Milton Br
Long Meadow

The Choakles
The Ashes

Road

2 Pr_ Lodge
Fa_

B526

Grange
Farm

The Grange

56

3

4

✝

**Preston
Deanery**

5

2 55

78 79

E F G H

Woott

E F G H

77 78

I Quinton Green

53

2

Courteenhall House

Home Farm

†

ourteenhall

East Lodge

Midshires Way

3

52

Fox Covert

4

ade

Cemetery

School

Bretts Lane

ll Road

Fox Covert Dr

The Grove

Midshires Way

5

Hartwell Road

251

As Fa

E F G H

77 78

Ro W

Ashton Lodge Farm

Abington.................52 A2
Abington Vale............52 C5
Bellinge.................41 H5
Blacky More..............68 A1
Blisworth................71 G4
Boothville...............40 B2
Boughton.................23 H4
Brackmills...............62 A4
Brafield-on-the-Green....64 C3
Briar Hill...............60 C1
Brixworth.................4 C4
Bugbrooke................57 C5
Chadstone................65 H5
Chapel Brampton..........21 G2
Church Brampton..........21 F4
Cogenhoe.................54 D4
Collingtree..............68 A4
Cotton End................2 C7
Courteenhall.............73 E2
Dallington...............50 B2
Denton...................65 F4

Duston...................49 G3
Earls Barton.............44 B4
East Hunsbury............60 C5
Ecton....................42 D5
Ecton Brook..............42 B5
Far Cotton...............60 D4
Farndish..................47 H1
Finedon...................8 A2
Gayton...................70 A2
Grange Park..............68 B5
Great Billing............41 H4
Great Brington...........34 D2
Great Doddington.........29 F5
Great Harrowden...........6 A4
Great Houghton...........62 D3
Hardingstone.............61 G4
Hardwick.................14 A1
Harlestone...............36 A5
Harpole..................48 A4
Hatton Park..............15 H3
Higham Ferrers...........19 G4

Hopping Hill.............49 G1
Hunsbury Hill............60 A3
Irchester................51 H5
Irthlingborough...........8 D3
King's Heath.............38 B5
Kingsley Park............51 H1
Kingsthorpe..............39 F3
Kingsthorpe Hollow.......51 F1
Kislingbury..............58 C1
Knuston..................32 B3
Little Billing...........41 G5
Little Brington..........34 C5
Little Houghton..........63 H1
Little Irchester.........50 C3
Little Wymington.........33 E5
Lower End................64 C2
Lower Harlestone.........36 D1
Meadow Vw................38 C2
Mears Ashby..............27 G2
Merefield................67 H1
Milton Malsor............67 F4

Moulton..................24 B4
Moulton Park.............39 H1
Nether Heyford...........56 C3
New Barton...............44 B2
New Duston...............37 E5
Northampton...............3 G4
Overstone................25 H3
Pitsford.................13 F5
Preston Deanery..........69 H4
Queen's Park.............38 D5
Raunds...................11 E2
Red Hill..................6 A5
Roade....................72 D4
Rothersthorpe............66 A3
Round Spinney............25 E5
Rushden..................33 E3
St James's End...........50 C5
Scaldwell.................5 H1
Shelfleys................60 A5
Spinney Hill.............39 H4
Stanwick.................10 C4

Strixton.................46
Sywell...................26
Upper Heyford............56
Upton Grange.............49
Warmonds Hill............19
Wellingborough...........25
West Hunsbury............60
Weston Favell............53
Whiston..................55
White Hills..............22
Wilby....................28
Wollaston................47
Wootton..................68

USING THE STREET INDEX

Street names are listed alphabetically. Each street name is followed by its postal town or area locality, the Postcode District, the page number, and the reference to the square in which the name is found.

Standard index entries are shown as follows:

Abbey Ri *BOZ/IR/WOL* NN29 ....**46** D2

Street names and selected addresses not shown on the map due to scale restrictions are shown in the index with an asterisk:

Barn Cnr *NHTNS* NN4 * **67** H4

GENERAL ABBREVIATIONS

ACC.................ACCESS
ALY..................ALLEY
AP................APPROACH
AR................ARCADE
ASS...........ASSOCIATION
AV.................AVENUE
BCH................BEACH
BLDS............BUILDINGS
BND..................BEND
BNK..................BANK
BR................BRIDGE
BRK................BROOK
BTM................BOTTOM
BUS..............BUSINESS
BVD.............BOULEVARD
BY..................BYPASS
CATH............CATHEDRAL
CEM..............CEMETERY
CEN................CENTRE
CFT.................CROFT
CH................CHURCH
CHA................CHASE
CHYD...........CHURCHYARD
CIR................CIRCLE
CIRC..............CIRCUS
CL.................CLOSE
CLFS..............CLIFFS
CMP.................CAMP
CNR................CORNER
CO................COUNTY
COLL.............COLLEGE
COM...............COMMON
COMM..........COMMISSION
CON..............CONVENT
COT...............COTTAGE
COTS............COTTAGES
CP.................CAPE
CPS................COPSE
CR................CREEK
CREM.........CREMATORIUM
CRS.............CRESCENT
CSWY...........CAUSEWAY
CT.................COURT
CTRL.............CENTRAL
CTS...............COURTS

CTYD...........COURTYARD
CUTT............CUTTINGS
CV..................COVE
CYN..............CANYON
DEPT.........DEPARTMENT
DL..................DALE
DM..................DAM
DRO................DROVE
DRY..............DRIVEWAY
DWGS..........DWELLINGS
E....................EAST
EMB...........EMBANKMENT
EMBY.............EMBASSY
ESP............ESPLANADE
EST................ESTATE
EX..............EXCHANGE
EXPY..........EXPRESSWAY
EXT.............EXTENSION
F/O..............FLYOVER
FC...........FOOTBALL CLUB
FK..................FORK
FLD................FIELD
FLDS..............FIELDS
FLS................FALLS
FLS................FLATS
FM..................FARM
FT..................FORT
FWY..............FREEWAY
FY.................FERRY
GA.................GATE
GAL..............GALLERY
GDN..............GARDEN
GDNS...........GARDENS
GLD................GLADE
GLN................GLEN
GN................GREEN
GND..............GROUND
GRA..............GRANGE
GRG..............GARAGE
GT................GREAT
GTWY............GATEWAY
GV................GROVE
HGR...............HIGHER
HL..................HILL

HLS................HILLS
HO................HOUSE
HOL..............HOLLOW
HOSP...........HOSPITAL
HRB.............HARBOUR
HTH................HEATH
HTS..............HEIGHTS
HVN................HAVEN
HWY.............HIGHWAY
IMP..............IMPERIAL
IN..................INLET
IND EST....INDUSTRIAL ESTATE
INF..............INFIRMARY
INFO..........INFORMATION
INT...........INTERCHANGE
IS................ISLAND
JCT.............JUNCTION
JTY.................JETTY
KG.................KING
KNL................KNOLL
L....................LAKE
LA.................LANE
LDG...............LODGE
LGT................LIGHT
LK.................LOCK
LKS................LAKES
LNDG.............LANDING
LTL................LITTLE
LWR................LOWER
MAG..........MAGISTRATE
MAN.............MANSIONS
MD.................MEAD
MDW............MEADOWS
MEM............MEMORIAL
MKT...............MARKET
MKTS............MARKETS
ML..................MALL
ML..................MILL
MNR................MANOR
MS.................MEWS
MSN..............MISSION
MT.................MOUNT
MTN............MOUNTAIN
MTS..........MOUNTAINS
MUS.............MUSEUM

MWY............MOTORWAY
N.................NORTH
NE...........NORTH EAST
NW...........NORTH WEST
O/P.............OVERPASS
OFF...............OFFICE
ORCH............ORCHARD
OV..................OVAL
PAL..............PALACE
PAS..............PASSAGE
PAV..............PAVILION
PDE..............PARADE
PH................PUBLIC HOUSE
PK..................PARK
PKWY............PARKWAY
PL.................PLACE
PLN................PLAIN
PLNS..............PLAINS
PLZ................PLAZA
POL........POLICE STATION
PR................PRINCE
PREC...........PRECINCT
PREP.........PREPARATORY
PRIM............PRIMARY
PROM.........PROMENADE
PRS............PRINCESS
PT.................PORT
PT................POINT
PTH................PATH
PZ.................PIAZZA
QD.............QUADRANT
QU................QUEEN
QY................QUAY
R..................RIVER
RBT.........ROUNDABOUT
RD.................ROAD
RDG................RIDGE
REP............REPUBLIC
RES...........RESERVOIR
RFC......RUGBY FOOTBALL CLUB
RI..................RISE
RP................RAMP
RW.................ROW
S.................SOUTH
SCH..............SCHOOL

SE................SOUTH E
SER...........SERVICE A
SH................SH
SHOP............SHOP
SKWY............SKY
SMT...............SUM
SOC...............SOC
SP................SP
SPR................SP
SQ................SQU
ST................STR
STN..............STA
STR................STR
STRD..............STR
SW.............SOUTH V
TDG..............TRAD
TER................TERR
THWY........THROUGH
TNL................TUN
TOLL.............TOLL
TPK................TURN
TR..................TR
TRL................T
U/P..........UNDERP
UNI............UNIVER
UP..................UP
V....................V
VA..................VA
VIAD..............VIAD
VIL..................V
VIS..................V
VLG................VIL
VW.................V
W...................W
WD.................W
WHF..............WH
WKS...............WA
WLS...............WE
WY..................Y.
YD..................Y.
YHA.........YOUTH HOS

POSTCODE TOWNS AND AREA ABBREVIATIONS

BOZ/IR/WOL.......Bozeat/Irchester/
                        Wollaston
BRIX/LBKBY.......Brixworth/
                        Long Buckby

IR/RAU/FIN........Irthlingborough/
                        Raunds/Finedon
NHTN................Northampton

NHTNE/MOU........Northampton east/
                        Moulton
NHTN/BOU......Northampton north/
                        Boughton

NHTNS...........Northampton south
NHTNW..........Northampton west
RKET..............Rural Kettering
RNHPTN........Rural Northampton

RSHD/HF.............Rusha
                    Higham Ferr
TOW.................Towce
WBORO.........Wellingboro

Index - streets   **Abb - Ant**

A

Abbey Ri *BOZ/IR/WOL* NN29....46 D2
Abbey Rd *NHTNS* NN4.......60 D2
  RNHPTN NN7.............72 C4
  WBORO NN8.............29 H2
Abbey St *NHTNW* NN5......50 C4
Abbey Wy *RSHD/HF* NN10....33 E4
Abbots Wy *NHTNW* NN5......50 B4
  RNHPTN NN7.............72 C4
  RSHD/HF NN10..........32 C5
Aberdare Rd *NHTNW* NN5....15 H5
Abington Av *NHTN* NN1......50 C2
Abington Park Crs
  NHTNE/MOU NN3..........51 H2
Abington Sq *NHTN* NN1......52 C3
Abington St *NHTN* NN1........3 C2
Abington St *NHTN* NN1........2 E3

Abthorpe Av *NHTNN/BOU* NN2....39 F2
Ace La *RNHPTN* NN7.........57 F5
Acre La *NHTN/BOU* NN2......38 C2
Adams Av *NHTN* NN1.........51 H5
Adams Ct *IR/RAU/FIN* NN9....10 C3
  WBORO NN8...............16 B4
Addington Rd *IR/RAU/FIN* NN9....9 G3
Addison Rd *NHTNE/MOU* NN5....40 A5
Addlecroft Cl *NHTNN/BOU* NN2....38 D4
Adelaide St *NHTNW/BOU* NN2....51 E5
Adit Vw *IR/RAU/FIN* NN9......18 B1
Adnitt Rd *NHTN* NN1.........51 H3
  RSHD/HF NN10..........33 E2
Affleck Br *IR/RAU/FIN* NN9.....7 H2
Aggate Wy *BRIX/LBKBY* NN6....43 H4
Agnes Rd *NHTN* NN2.........51 E2
Ainsdale Cl *NHTNN/BOU* NN2....39 H4
Aintree Dr *RSHD/HF* NN10.....2 B4
Aintree Rd *NHTNE/MOU* NN3....39 H3
Albany Rd *NHTN* NN1.........52 A3
Albert Pl *NHTN* NN1.........52 D2

Albert Rd *IR/RAU/FIN* NN9.......7 H1
  RSHD/HF NN10...........33 F2
Albion Ms *WBORO* NN8.......16 B4
Albion Pl *NHTN* NN1.........3 E4
  RSHD/HF NN10...........33 F1
Alcombe Rd *NHTN* NN1........3 F2
Alcombe Ter *NHTN* NN1........3 G1
Alder Ct *NHTNE/MOU* NN5......4 A1
Alderley Cl *NHTNW* NN5......49 F2
Aldsworth Cl *WBORO* NN8....29 C4
Aldwell St *NHTNS* NN4.......52 B5
Alexander Ct *NHTNE/MOU* NN3....41 E4
Alexander Rd *IR/RAU/FIN* NN9....9 G2
Alexandra Pl *IR/RAU/FIN* NN9....9 G2
Alexandra Rd *NHTN* NN1......33 H2
  RSHD/HF NN10...........33 F2
  WBORO NN8...............16 B4
Alfred St *BOZ/IR/WOL* NN29....31 H4
  IR/RAU/FIN NN9..........10 B4
  NHTN NN1................3 J5
  RSHD/HF NN10...........33 F2

Alibone Cl *NHTNE/MOU* NN3....24 D3
Alington Cl *IR/RAU/FIN* NN9.....8 A1
Alken Cl *WBORO* NN8........15 H1
Allard Cl *NHTNE/MOU* NN5....42 B2
Allebone Rd *BRIX/LBKBY* NN6....44 A4
Allen Rd *IR/RAU/FIN* NN9......8 H1
  IR/RAU/FIN NN9..........9 E5
  NHTN NN1................51 H3
  RSHD/HF NN10...........33 H1
Alliance Ter *WBORO* NN8.....15 H4
Alliston Gdns
  NHTNN/BOU NN2..........51 E3
Alma St *NHTNW* NN5.........50 C4
  WBORO NN8...............16 A4
Almond Crs *RNHPTN* NN7......57 H5
Alpine Rd *RSHD/HF* NN10.....32 D2
Alpine Wy *NHTNW* NN5........37 E4
Alsace Cl *NHTNW* NN5........48 D1
Althorp Cl *WBORO* NN8......15 E2
Althorp Rd *NHTNW* NN5......50 C4
Althorp St *NHTN* NN5.........2 C5

Alton St *NHTNS* NN4.........60
Alvis Ct *NHTNE/MOU* NN3......4 E2
Ambleside Cl
  NHTNE/MOU NN3..........4
  WBORO NN8..............
Ambridge Cl *NHTNS* NN4......64
Ambush St *NHTNW* NN5........5
Anchor Dr *NHTNN/BOU* NN2....38
Andrew Cl *RSHD/HF* NN10.....1
Andrews Wy *IR/RAU/FIN* NN9....1
Angel La *WBORO* NN8........
Angel St *NHTN* NN1.........
Anglia Wy *RSHD/HF* NN10.....3
Anjou Ct *NHTNW* NN5........
Anne Cl *RSHD/HF* NN10......5
Anne Rd *WBORO* NN8.........
Annesley Cl *NHTNE/MOU* NN5....5
Ansell Wy *NHTNS* NN4.......
Antona Cl *IR/RAU/FIN* NN9....
Antona Dr *IR/RAU/FIN* NN9....
Antona Gdns *IR/RAU/FIN* NN9....

RNHPTN NN7 ....72 D4
RSHD/HF NN10 ....19 F4
RSHD/HF NN10 ....33 F2
WBORO NN8 ....15 H4
High St South RSHD/HF NN10...33 F5
High Vw NHTNS NN4................58 B4
High Woods BRIX/LBKBY NN6...26 B4
Hillary Rd RSHD/HF NN10 ....32 D3
Hillberry Ri RSHD/HF NN3........42 B3
Hill Cl NHTNW NN5................37 G5
Hill Crest RNHPTN NN7...........71 E2
Hillcrest Av NHTNE/MOU NN3....40 A4
Hillcrest Rd RNHPTN NN7........70 A2
Hilldrop Rd NHTNS NN4...........67 G1
Hill Farm Ri NHTNS NN4..........60 B5
Hill House Gdns
    IR/RAU/FIN NN9.................10 B5
Hillside Crs RNHPTN NN7.........56 C3
Hillside Rd RNHPTN NN7..........56 C3
Hillside Ter NHTNE/MOU NN3....16 C2
Hillside Wy NHTNE/MOU NN3....52 C2
Hill St IR/RAU/FIN NN9 ....11 F2
    WBORO NN8 ....15 H5
The Hill NHTNS NN4...............63 E3
Hilltop RNHPTN NN7...............71 E2
Hilltop Cl BRIX/LBKBY NN6.......4 D5
Hind Stile RSHD/HF NN10........33 F3
Hinton Cl NHTNU/BOU NN2.......39 E2
Hinton Rd NHTNU/BOU NN2......39 E2
Hinwick Rd BOZ/IR/WOL NN29...46 D5
Hirondelle Cl NHTNW NN5.........48 B1
Hobby Cl NHTNS NN4.............60 D5
Hocknell Cl NHTNS NN4...........68 D2
Hodges La RNHPTN NN7..........58 B1
Hodnet Cl NHTNS NN4............68 A1
Hoe Wy RNHPTN NN7.............72 C4
Holbein Gdns NHTNS NN4........60 A5
Holbush Wy IR/RAU/FIN NN9......9 E3
Holcot Cl WBORO NN8.............15 G1
Holcot Rd BRIX/LBKBY NN6......4 D4
    NHTNE/MOU NN3..............68 D1
Holcutt Cl NHTNS NN4............68 D1
Holdenby Rd NHTNU/BOU NN2...39 D4
The Hollies NHTNE/MOU NN3....24 B2
    WBORO NN8 ....15 G1
Hollingside Dr NHTNU/BOU NN2.39 D4
Hollington Rd IR/RAU/FIN NN9...11 F2
Hollow Bank NHTNE/MOU NN3...40 C1
Holly Lodge Dr
    NHTNU/BOU NN2...............39 F1
Holly Rd NHTN NN1...............51 E2
    RSHD/HF NN10.................52 C1
Holly Wk IR/RAU/FIN NN9..........7 G2
Holman Cl NHTNE/MOU NN3.....40 D5
Holme Cl IR/RAU/FIN NN9..........6 A5
Holmecross Rd
    NHTNE/MOU NN3..............41 E2
Holmes Av IR/RAU/FIN NN9......11 F3
Holmfield Dr IR/RAU/FIN NN9....11 G2
Holmfield Wy NHTNE/MOU NN3..41 E2
Holmleigh Cl NHTNW NN5........49 G3
Holmwood Cl NHTNW NN5.......49 E1
Holyoake Rd BOZ/IR/WOL NN29..46 D3
Holyrood Rd NHTNW NN5.........50 B3
Home Acre RNHPTN NN7.........63 H2
Home Cl RNHPTN NN7............71 F4
Home Farm Cl
    NHTNE/MOU NN3..............53 H2
Homestead Cl
    NHTNE/MOU NN3..............51 G1
Homestead Dr RNHPTN NN7.....57 G5
Homestead Ri NHTNS NN4........68 C2
Homestead Wy
    NHTNU/BOU NN2...............51 G1
Honey Holme BRIX/LBKBY NN6...4 A5
Honeystones NHTNE/MOU NN3..24 C3
Honeysuckle Wy
    NHTNE/MOU NN3..............52 C4
Hood St NHTN NN1...............51 G3
Hookhams Pth
    BOZ/IR/WOL NN29.............47 E3
Hopes Pl NHTNU/BOU NN2.......38 D4
Hopmeadow Ct
    NHTNE/MOU NN3..............41 H3
Hopping Hill Gdns NHTNW NN5..55 F4
Hornbeam Cl WBORO NN8.......15 G4
Hornbeam Ct NHTNE/MOU NN3..15 G4
Hornby Rd BRIX/LBKBY NN6.....44 A2
Horse Market NHTN NN1.........2 C4
Horsemarket NHTN NN1..........2 C4
Horsemoor Sq
    NHTNE/MOU NN3..............42 A5
Horseshoe Cl BRIX/LBKBY NN6...5 E4
Horseshoe St NHTN NN1..........2 C4
Horse Well Ct NHTNE/MOU NN3..58 A5
Horsley Rd NHTNU/BOU NN2.....50 D1
Horton Rd RNHPTN NN7..........64 B4
Houghton HI NHTNS NN4.........61 H4
Hove Rd RSHD/HF NN10..........33 G2
Howard Biley Gdns
    NHTNE/MOU NN3..............40 C3
Howard La NHTNE/MOU NN3.....23 E5
Howard Rd BOZ/IR/WOL NN29...46 D5
Hoylake WBORO NN8.............15 E2
Hoylake Dr NHTNU/BOU NN2....39 H4
Hudson Dr NHTNS NN4...........59 H4
Hulme Wy WBORO NN8..........15 G4
Humber Dr NHTNW NN5..........38 A5
Humber Gdns NHTNE/MOU NN3..15 G4
Humfrey La NHTNU/BOU NN2....23 E3
Hunsbarrow Rd NHTNS NN4......60 A2
Hunsbury Cl NHTNS NN4..........60 A4
Hunsbury Gn NHTNS NN4.........59 H3
Hunsbury Hill Av NHTNS NN4.....60 A4
Hunsbury Hill Rd NHTNS NN4....60 A4
Hunslet La NHTNS NN4...........60 A4
Hunt Cl BRIX/LBKBY NN6.........4 A4
    WBORO NN8 ....15 H1
Hunters Cl NHTNU/BOU NN2.....42 A4
Hunters' Wy BRIX/LBKBY NN6....4 D4
Huntsham Cl NHTNE/MOU NN3..52 D3
Huntsmead NHTNE/MOU NN3....42 A4
Huxley Cl WBORO NN8...........14 C5
Huxloe Ri NHTNE/MOU NN3......14 C2
Hyacinth Wy RSHD/HF NN10.....33 F5

Hyde Cl RNHPTN NN7.............72 C4
Hyde Dr IR/RAU/FIN NN9..........8 A1
Hyde Rd RNHPTN NN7............72 C4

I

Ibstock Cl NHTNE/MOU NN3.....41 G1
Icknield Dr NHTNS NN4...........60 A4
Ilex Cl NHTNS NN4................61 H4
Ilmor Av BRIX/LBKBY NN6........5 E3
Indmere Ct NHTNS NN4...........59 G4
Inglewood Ct NHTNE/MOU NN3..54 A1
Insignia Cl NHTNS NN4...........48 A2
Irchester Rd BOZ/IR/WOL NN29..47 C2
    RSHD/HF NN10.................32 C2
Iron Pikes BRIX/LBKBY NN6......5 E4
Ironstone La NHTNS NN4.........60 A2
Ironstone Wy BRIX/LBKBY NN6...5 E2
Irthlingborough Rd
    IR/RAU/FIN NN9.................8 A2
    WBORO NN8 ....30 B1
Isham Cl NHTNU/BOU NN2.......39 F2
Ivy La IR/RAU/FIN NN9...........39 F2
Ivy Rd NHTN NN1.................51 H2
Ixworth Cl NHTNE/MOU NN3.....37 F2

J

Jackdaw Cl NHTNE/MOU NN3....54 A2
Jacklin Ct WBORO NN8...........15 E2
Jackson Cl NHTNU/BOU NN2.....39 D5
Jackson's La NHTNS NN4.........15 H5
Jacorrin Cl NHTNU/BOU NN2.....39 G1
James Lewis Ct
    NHTNE/MOU NN3..............40 C5
James Rd WBORO NN8...........30 A3
James St BOZ/IR/WOL NN29......31 H5
Jardine Cl NHTNE/MOU NN3.....52 D1
Jarretts Yd NHTNS NN4..........68 C2
Jasmine Gdns RSHD/HF NN10...33 F5
Jasmine Rd NHTNE/MOU NN3....52 A2
Javelin Cl NHTNW NN5...........49 G2
Jenner Crs NHTNE/MOU NN3....38 D2
Jennings Cl RSHD/HF NN10......19 F4
Jersey Cl WBORO NN8............15 F1
Jersey Cr NHTNS NN4............53 F1
Jeyes Cl NHTNE/MOU NN3.......24 B3
Joan Pyel Cl IR/RAU/FIN NN9....18 C1
John Gray Rd
    BOZ/IR/WOL NN29.............45 F1
John Lea Wy WBORO NN8........29 H3
John Pyel Rd IR/RAU/FIN NN9....9 E5
Johnson Ct NHTNS NN4..........37 G4
Johns Rd RNHPTN NN7..........57 G4
John St RSHD/HF NN10..........33 F2
Joshua Sq NHTNS NN4...........60 B2
Jubilee Cl NHTN NN1.............60 B2
Jubilee Crs WBORO NN8.........29 H2
Jubilee St IR/RAU/FIN NN9.......9 G5
Julian Wy NHTNU/BOU NN2......51 G1
Junction Rd NHTNU/BOU NN2....39 E4
Juniper Ct NHTNE/MOU NN3.....42 B4
Juniper Thorn BRIX/LBKBY NN6..5 E5

K

Kangaroo Spinney WBORO NN8..30 D1
Kealdale Rd NHTNE/MOU NN3...40 A3
Keats Cl BRIX/LBKBY NN6........44 B4
    NHTNS NN4 ....60 B5
Keats Rd NHTNE/MOU NN3......15 F5
Keats Wy RSHD/HF NN10........32 C2
Kedleston Cl NHTNS NN4........61 E5
Keepers Cl NHTNS NN4..........68 D5
Kelburn Cl NHTNS NN4..........49 G1
Kelmscott Cl NHTNE/MOU NN3..41 G2
Kelsall Cl NHTNW NN5............49 F2
Kendal Cl NHTNE/MOU NN3......40 D3
    RSHD/HF NN10................33 G3
    WBORO NN8 ....33 G3
Kenilworth Cl NHTNW NN5.......49 F2
    RSHD/HF NN10................33 G3
Kenmuir Av NHTNU/BOU NN2....39 H5
Kenmuir Crs NHTNU/BOU NN2...39 H5
Kenmuir Gdns
    NHTNU/BOU NN2...............39 H5
Kennel Ter BRIX/LBKBY NN6.....4 D4
Kennet Cl WBORO NN8...........14 D3
Kennet Gn NHTNW NN5..........38 B5
Kensington Cl RSHD/HF NN10....32 C1
Kent Cl NHTNW NN5.............49 C4
Kentford Cl NHTNS NN4..........60 D5
Kent Rd NHTNW NN5.............49 E4
    RSHD/HF NN10................33 G1
Kentstone Cl NHTNU/BOU NN2..38 B2
Kerrfield Est NHTNS NN4.........49 G2
Keston Wy NHTNE/MOU NN3....10 D5
Kestrel Cl NHTNW NN5...........52 D1
Kestrel La WBORO NN8..........16 A2
Keswick Dr NHTNE/MOU NN3....53 H1
    RSHD/HF NN10................33 H1
Kettering Gdns NHTN NN1.......3 G2
Kettering Rd IR/RAU/FIN NN9....6 A2
    NHTN NN1 ....51 H1
    NHTNE/MOU NN3..............49 E2
    NHTNS NN4 ....60 A4
Kettering Rd North
    NHTN NN1 ....40 C3
Keyham Ct NHTNE/MOU NN3....41 G2
Keystone NHTNS NN4............46 D3
Kilborn Cl WBORO NN8..........15 F3
Kilborn Rd WBORO NN8..........15 F3
Kilburn Pl RSHD/HF NN10........15 F5
Kilby Cl NHTNE/MOU NN3........29 F1

Kilnway WBORO NN8.............15 F5
Kilvey Rd NHTNS NN4............62 A3
Kimble Cl NHTNS NN4............60 D5
Kimbolton Rd RSHD/HF NN10....19 G3
King Edward Rd NHTN NN1......52 A3
Kingfisher Cl NHTNS NN4........68 A5
Kingfisher Ct BRIX/LBKBY NN6..26 B4
Kingmaker Wy NHTNS NN4......60 C3
King Richard Ct NHTNS NN4.....60 A2
Kings Av RSHD/HF NN10.........19 G2
Kings Cl NHTNS NN4.............68 D5
Kingscroft Ct NHTNE/MOU NN3..54 A1
Kingsfield Cl NHTNS NN4.........50 C1
Kingsfield Wy NHTNS NN4........50 B1
Kingsland Av NHTNE/MOU NN3..39 E4
Kingsland Cl NHTNU/BOU NN2...39 F4
Kingsland Gdns
    NHTNU/BOU NN2...............39 E4
Kingsley Gdns NHTNU/BOU NN2.51 G1
Kingsley Rd NHTNU/BOU NN2....51 G1
Kingsmead NHTNE/MOU NN3....38 C2
Kings Meadow La
    RSHD/HF NN10.................19 F2
Kingsmead Pk RSHD/HF NN10...33 G5
Kingsmith Dr IR/RAU/FIN NN9...11 G2
Kings Park Rd
    NHTNE/MOU NN3..............39 H1
Kings Pl RSHD/HF NN10.........33 G2
Kings Rd RSHD/HF NN10.........33 G2
Kings St WBORO NN8............16 A4
Kingsthorpe Gv
    NHTNU/BOU NN2...............39 E5
Kingsthorpe Rd
    NHTNU/BOU NN2...............51 E1
King St BRIX/LBKBY NN6.........44 A2
Kingsway NHTNU/BOU NN2......38 D5
    WBORO NN8 ....29 G2
Kingswell Rd NHTNU/BOU NN2..38 D4
Kingswell St NHTN NN1...........2 D4
Kinross Cl NHTNE/MOU NN3.....53 F2
Kirby Cl NHTNS NN4.............68 D1
Kirton Cl NHTNE/MOU NN3......41 H3
Kirton End NHTNE/MOU NN3....41 H3
Kislingbury Rd RNHPTN NN7.....57 G4
Kites Cl NHTN NN1...............48 A2
Knaphill Crs NHTNS NN4.........60 B1
Knightlands Rd IR/RAU/FIN NN9..9 H3
Knightley Rd NHTNU/BOU NN2...51 E1
Knighton Cl NHTNW NN5.........37 E4
Knightons Wy BRIX/LBKBY NN6..5 E3
Knightscliffe Wy NHTNW NN5....49 H1
Knights Cl BRIX/LBKBY NN6......44 A2
Knights Ct NHTNS NN4...........53 C1
    NHTNE/MOU NN3..............15 H4
Knight's La NHTNU/BOU NN2....38 D4
The Knoll BRIX/LBKBY NN6......5 E4
Knowle Cl NHTNE/MOU NN3.....52 C4
Knowles Ct RSHD/HF NN10......33 H1
Knox Rd WBORO NN8............16 B5
Kyoto Cl NHTNE/MOU NN3......39 H1

L

Laburnham Cl WBORO NN8......15 G4
Laburnum Crs
    NHTNE/MOU NN3..............40 A5
Ladybridge Dr NHTNS NN4.......59 H5
Lady Hollow Dr NHTNS NN4......60 A5
Ladymead Cl NHTNS NN4........59 H4
Lady's La BRIX/LBKBY NN6.......27 F2
    NHTN NN1 ....2 D2
Lady Winefride's Wk
    NHTNE/MOU NN3..............41 H5
The Lakes NHTNS NN4...........62 C1
Lakeside IR/RAU/FIN NN9........18 B1
    NHTNS NN4 ....25 C5
    NHTNS NN4 ....68 A5
Lakeside Dr NHTNE/MOU NN3...42 B4
Lake Wk NHTNS NN4............68 A5
Lambrook Dr NHTNS NN4........68 A1
Lancaster Cl BOZ/IR/WOL NN29..46 C2
Lancaster St RSHD/HF NN10.....19 G3
Lancaster Wy NHTNS NN4.......60 C3
    RSHD/HF NN10................33 F2
Landcross Dr NHTNE/MOU NN3..53 C2
Landimore Rd NHTNS NN4.......69 E1
Landsdown Dr
    NHTNE/MOU NN3..............41 E5
Lanercost Wk NHTNE/MOU NN3..40 C3
Laneside Hollow NHTNS NN4.....68 A2
The Lane RNHPTN NN7..........65 F5
    RNHPTN NN7 ....66 B2
Langdale Rd NHTNE/MOU NN3..39 E5
Langford Dr NHTNS NN4.........68 B5
Langham Rd IR/RAU/FIN NN9....9 G5
Langley Cl NHTNS NN4...........59 H2
Langley Crs NHTNS NN4.........9 H1
Langsett Cl NHTNE/MOU NN3...53 F1
Lapwing Cl NHTNS NN4..........67 G1
Larch Cl BOZ/IR/WOL NN29......31 F5
Larch La NHTNW NN5............55 F2
Larchwood Cl WBORO NN8......15 G4
Larkhall La NHTNS NN4..........48 A4
Larkhall Wy RNHPTN NN7.......48 A3
Larkhill RSHD/HF NN10..........19 E5
Larkin Gdns RSHD/HF NN10.....18 D4
Lark La NHTNS NN4.............68 D4
Lark Ri NHTNE/MOU NN3........41 G3
Larwood Ct NHTNE/MOU NN3...38 C2
Lasham Ct NHTNE/MOU NN3....54 A1
Latymer Ct NHTN NN1...........17 F2
Lauderdale Av NHTNS NN4.......60 C3
Launcelot Ct NHTNS NN4........49 E5
Laurel Cl NHTNE/MOU NN3......41 E4
The Laurels BRIX/LBKBY NN6....42 D4
    NHTNE/MOU NN3..............24 B2
Laurel Va NHTNS NN4...........68 D2
Lavant Wk NHTNE/MOU NN3....39 H2
Lavender Wy RSHD/HF NN10....33 G4
Lavenham Cl NHTNE/MOU NN3..41 F2
The Lawns NHTNW NN5.........50 A2

Lawrence Cl IR/RAU/FIN NN9....10 D4
Lawrence Ct NHTN NN1.........51 E3
Laws La IR/RAU/FIN NN9.........7 H2
Lawson Crs NHTNE/MOU NN3...11 F2
Lawton Cl NHTNE/MOU NN3.....40 A3
Lawton Rd IR/RAU/FIN NN9......33 C1
Laywood Cl IR/RAU/FIN NN9.....11 E1
Laywood Wy IR/RAU/FIN NN9....18 C1
Leafields NHTNE/MOU NN3......53 F2
Lean Bank NHTNS NN4..........60 C3
Lea Rd NHTN NN1...............51 H2
Lea Wy WBORO NN8............15 F5
Leben Sq NHTNE/MOU NN3.....42 A2
Ledaig Wy NHTNE/MOU NN3....40 A3
Lees St IR/RAU/FIN NN9..........9 E5
Lee Wy IR/RAU/FIN NN9.........11 F1
Leicester St NHTNE/MOU NN3...51 E3
Leicester Ter
    NHTNE/MOU NN3..............51 E3
Leighton Cl WBORO NN8........15 H2
Leonard La NHTNE/MOU NN3....24 C3
Leslie Rd NHTNU/BOU NN2......50 D5
Lesson Rd BRIX/LBKBY NN6.....60 D2
Letts Rd NHTNS NN4............60 D2
Levitts Rd RNHPTN NN7.........58 B2
Lichfield Dr NHTNS NN4.........67 G1
Liddington Wy
    NHTNU/BOU NN2...............38 D2
Lilac Cl WBORO NN8............15 G4
Lilac Gv RSHD/HF NN10.........33 F5
Lilford Av NHTNU/BOU NN2.....53 F2
Lilley Ter IR/RAU/FIN NN9........9 F4
Lime Av NHTNE/MOU NN3.......52 A1
Lime Farm Wy NHTNS NN4......63 E5
Limefields Wy NHTNS NN4......68 D2
Lime Gv RNHPTN NN7...........58 B5
    WBORO NN8 ....16 A2
Limehurst Cl NHTNW NN5.......49 F1
Limehurst Rd NHTNW NN5......49 G2
Lime St IR/RAU/FIN NN9.........11 F1
Lime Ter IR/RAU/FIN NN9........9 F4
Limlow Cl NHTNS NN4...........59 H2
Limoges Ct NHTNW NN5........37 E5
Linacre Cl NHTNE/MOU NN3.....41 F1
Lincoln Rd NHTNW NN5.........50 C5
Lincoln St NHTNE/MOU NN3.....38 D4
Lindale Cl NHTNE/MOU NN3.....40 B4
Linden Av RSHD/HF NN10.......19 F2
Linden Rd NHTNE/MOU NN3.....52 A1
Lindisfarne Wy NHTNS NN4......68 B5
Lindsay Av NHTNE/MOU NN3....40 A5
Lindsay Ter NHTNE/MOU NN3...40 A5
Lings Wy NHTNE/MOU NN3.....41 G3
Lingswood Pk
    NHTNE/MOU NN3..............41 G4
Link Rd NHTNE/MOU NN3.......38 C1
    RSHD/HF NN10................33 F5
Links Rd WBORO NN8...........16 C1
Link Wy RNHPTN NN7...........57 G5
Linley Gn NHTNW NN5..........49 H2
Linnett Cl NHTNS NN4..........53 H2
Linnetts La RSHD/HF NN10......19 F4
Lismore Cl NHTNE/MOU NN3....42 A5
Lister Dr NHTNS NN4............60 A4
Lister Rd WBORO NN8...........16 A4
Little Billing Wy
    NHTNE/MOU NN3..............41 G5
Little Cl BRIX/LBKBY NN6........21 H3
Little Cross St NHTN NN1........2 B3
Littledale WBORO NN8..........15 F3
Little Fld NHTNS NN4............68 D4
Little Greeve Wy NHTNS NN4....49 E3
Little Gull Cl NHTNE/MOU NN3...41 F1
Little La BOZ/IR/WOL NN29......46 D2
    NHTNS NN4 ....63 E3
    NHTNS NN4 ....71 F5
Little Park St NHTNE/MOU NN3..38 D4
Little St RSHD/HF NN10.........33 G3
Littlewood Cl NHTNW NN5......50 C2
Lloyd Cl WBORO NN8...........16 B1
Lockcroft Sq
    NHTNE/MOU NN3..............42 B5
Lockwood Ct NHTNE/MOU NN3..38 D5
Lodge Av NHTNS NN4...........68 A4
Lodge Cl NHTNS NN4...........68 D5
    NHTNW NN5 ....49 F1
    RNHPTN NN7 ....69 G1
Lodge Rd RNHPTN NN7..........69 G1
    RSHD/HF NN10................37 H4
Lodge Wy IR/RAU/FIN NN9......18 C1
    NHTNW NN5 ....37 G4
Logwell Ct NHTNE/MOU NN3....53 F1
Loire Cl NHTNW NN5...........37 F5
Lombardy Ct NHTNE/MOU NN3..37 H3
London End BOZ/IR/WOL NN29..31 H5
    BRIX/LBKBY NN6..............44 A3
London Rd BOZ/IR/WOL NN29...46 D4
    IR/RAU/FIN NN9...............11 F2
    NHTNS NN4 ....68 B5
    RNHPTN NN7 ....72 C4
    WBORO NN8 ....30 B1
Lone Pine Ct BRIX/LBKBY NN6...4 D4
Long Acre RNHPTN NN7.........64 B2
Long Acres NHTNS NN4.........68 D2
Long Acres Dr RSHD/HF NN10...19 E5
Longfellow Rd WBORO NN8.....14 C5
Longford Av NHTNE/MOU NN3...53 C2
Longland Ct NHTNE/MOU NN3..40 B5
Longland Rd NHTNE/MOU NN3..40 B5

Longleat Ct NHTNE/MOU NN4
    NHTNE/MOU NN3
Long Mallows Ri
    NHTNE/MOU NN3
Long Marsh Sq
    NHTNE/MOU NN3
Longmead Ct NHTNE/MOU NN4
Long Meadow NHTNS NN4
Long Mynd Dr NHTNW NN5
Longueville Ct
    NHTNE/MOU NN3
Lordswood Cl NHTNS NN4
Lorne Rd NHTN NN1
Lorraine Crs NHTNE/MOU NN3
Lorraine Dr NHTNE/MOU NN3
Loseby Cl RSHD/HF NN10
Louisberg Cl NHTNS NN4
Louisburg Cl NHTNS NN4
Louise Rd NHTN NN1
Louth Dr RSHD/HF NN10
Lovat Dr NHTNW NN5
Lovell Cl IR/RAU/FIN NN9
Lovell Rd IR/RAU/FIN NN9
Lower Adelaide St
    NHTNU/BOU NN2
Lower Bath St NHTN NN1
Lower Ecton La
    NHTNE/MOU NN3
Lower Farm Rd
    NHTNE/MOU NN3
Lower Harding St NHTN NN1
Lower Hester St
    NHTNU/BOU NN2
Lower Meadow Ct
    NHTNE/MOU NN3
Lower Mounts NHTN NN1
Lower Priory St NHTN NN1
Lower Rd RNHPTN NN7
Lower St BOZ/IR/WOL NN29
Lower Thrift St NHTN NN1
Low Farm Pl NHTNE/MOU NN3
Low Greeve NHTNS NN4
Lowick Cl WBORO NN8
Lowick Ct NHTNE/MOU NN3
Lowlands Cl NHTNE/MOU NN3
Lowry Cl WBORO NN8
Loxton Cl NHTNW NN5
Loyd Rd NHTN NN1
Lucas Cl IR/RAU/FIN NN9
Ludlow Cl NHTNE/MOU NN3
Lumbertubs La
    NHTNE/MOU NN3
Lumbertubs Ri
    NHTNE/MOU NN3
Lumbertubs Wy
    NHTNE/MOU NN3
Lunchfield La NHTNE/MOU NN3
Lundie Cl IR/RAU/FIN NN9
Lutterworth Rd NHTN NN1
Lydia Ct RSHD/HF NN10
Lyle Ct WBORO NN8
Lyncrest Av NHTNW NN5
Lyncroft Wy NHTNU/BOU NN2
Lyneford Wy BOZ/IR/WOL NN29
Lynmore Cl NHTNS NN4
Lynmouth Av NHTNE/MOU NN3
Lynton Av NHTNU/BOU NN2
Lytham Cl NHTNU/BOU NN2
Lytham Ct WBORO NN8
Lyttleton Rd NHTNW NN5
Lyveden Rd NHTNS NN4

M

Mackenzie Rd IR/RAU/FIN NN9
Mackworth Dr IR/RAU/FIN NN9
Maclean Cl NHTNE/MOU NN3
Macmillans Wy RNHPTN NN7
Macmillan Wy
Macon Cl NHTNW NN5
Magee St NHTN NN1
Magnolia Cl NHTNE/MOU NN3
Magnolia Dr RSHD/HF NN10
Maida Cl NHTNS NN4
Maidencastle NHTNE/MOU NN3
Main Rd BRIX/LBKBY NN6
    NHTNS NN4
    NHTNW NN5
    RNHPTN NN7
Main St RNHPTN NN7
Malcolm Dr NHTNW NN5
Malcolm Rd NHTNU/BOU NN2
Malcolm Ter NHTNU/BOU NN2
Malham Ct WBORO NN8
Mallard Cl BRIX/LBKBY NN6
Mallery Cl RSHD/HF NN10
Mallory Wk NHTNE/MOU NN3
Mallows Dr IR/RAU/FIN NN9
Malpas Dr RNHPTN NN7
The Maltings
    BOZ/IR/WOL NN29
Malvern Cl WBORO NN8
Malvern Gv NHTNW NN5
Malzor La RNHPTN NN7
Manchester Rd
    BOZ/IR/WOL NN29
Mander Cl RNHPTN NN7
Manfield Rd NHTN NN1
Manningham Rd
    IR/RAU/FIN NN9
Manning Rd NHTNE/MOU NN3
Mannings Ri RSHD/HF NN10
Mannington Gdns NHTNS NN4
Manor Acres NHTNE/MOU NN3
Manor Cl BOZ/IR/WOL NN29
    RNHPTN NN7
    RNHPTN NN7
Manor Ct RSHD/HF NN10
Manor Dr IR/RAU/FIN NN9

Farm Ct *RNHPTN* NN7 ....55 E4
Farm Rd
RAU/FIN NN3 ....11 G2
field Cl *NHTNE/MOU* NN3 ....41 H5
field Cl *NHTNE/MOU* NN3 ..53 H2
field Rd
TNE/MOU NN3 ....53 G2
Gdns *IR/RAU/FIN* NN3 ......10 C5
House Cl
X/LBKBY NN6 ....44 A2
house Gdns
TNE/MOU NN3 ....11 F2
La *BRIX/LBKBY* NN6 ....44 A2
Pk *RNHPTN* NN7 ....56 C2
Rd *BRIX/LBKBY* NN6 ....13 F4
X/LBKBY NN6 ....27 F2
TNE/MOU NN3 ....24 C4
/D/HF NN10 ....38 D4
ID/HF NN10 ....33 H4
St *IR/RAU/FIN* NN9 ....11 F2
Wy *RSHD/HF* NN10 ....19 G4
rd Cl *NHTNW* NN5 ....50 A4
field St *IR/RAU/FIN* NN9 ......8 B3
on Cl *NHTNE/MOU* NN3 ..40 A1
en Rd *IR/RAU/FIN* NN9 ....9 E4
ID/HF NN10 ....33 C3
Cl *RNHPTN* NN7 ....57 F5
Dr *WBORO* NN8 ....15 G4
Rd *RSHD/HF* NN10 ....33 C2
toft St *IR/RAU/FIN* NN9 ....11 E5
Wd *RSHD/HF* NN10 ....33 F4
erley Dr *NHTNE/MOU* NN5 ..55 F5
wood Cl
/TNE/MOU NN3 ....41 F1
ret Av *WBORO* NN8 ....2 B4
ret St *NHTN* NN1 ....2 E1
am Cl *NHTNS* NN4 ....68 B3
t Sq *NHTN* NN1 ....2 D3
t St *NHTN* NN1 ....3 H1
t Wk *NHTN* NN1 ....3 H1
am Cl *NHTNW* NN5 ....49 G1
Cl *IR/RAU/FIN* NN9 ....10 C5
rough Av *WBORO* NN8 ....15 F2
rough Rd *NHTNW* NN5 ....56 C4
ow Cl *NHTNS* NN4 ....67 G1
ones *NHTNS* NN4 ....58 H3
ck Sq *NHTNS* NN4 ....60 A5
dee Dr *NHTNE/MOU* NN3 ..53 E5
et *IR/RAU/FIN* NN9 ....12 A1
tt St *NHTN/BOU* NN2 ....51 E2
leys Ct *NHTNE/MOU* NN3 ..53 G2
ell Ct *NHTNE/MOU* NN3 ..55 G2
Cl *NHTNW* NN5 ....48 D1
Cl *RSHD/HF* NN10 ....19 E5
dale *NHTN/BOU* NN2 ....38 B2
s La *NHTNS* NN4 ....61 G5
s Yd *NHTNS* NN4 ....50 D5
od Cl *NHTNE/MOU* NN3 ..52 B3
ld Cl *WBORO* NN8 ....15 F2
ld Rd *RSHD/HF* NN10 ....33 H4
ld Wy *NHTNE/MOU* NN2 ..39 G5
y Cl *NHTNW* NN5 ....61 G5
ess Cl *NHTNW* NN5 ....49 E1
n Ct *IR/RAU/FIN* NN9 ....9 G4
Cl *RSHD/HF* NN10 ....33 C5
ld Rd *NHTNE/MOU* NN3 ..40 B4
bon Wk *IR/RAU/FIN* NN9 ..11 F1
es Wy *IR/RAU/FIN* NN9 ....11 F1
s Cl *NHTNW* NN5 ....56 C3
s La *NHTNS* NN4 ....19 E5
ORO NN8 ....16 D2
w Dr *RSHD/HF* NN10 ....10 C2
w La *IR/RAU/FIN* NN9 ....9 G5
HPTN NN7 ....57 G5
eadows *IR/RAU/FIN* NN9 ...6 A5
w Sweet Rd
ID/HF NN10 ....33 G5
bw Vw *RSHD/HF* NN10 ....19 E3
ow Wk *RSHD/HF* NN10 ....19 E3
sw Wy *IR/RAU/FIN* NN9 ....10 D4
way *NHTNE/MOU* NN3 ..53 G2
HPTN NN7 ....57 G5
Ashby Rd
X/LBKBY NN6 ....27 F5
ourne Cl *NHTNE/MOU* NN3 ..24 B5
iln Hl *NHTNE/MOU* NN3 ..41 F1
am Cl *NHTNS* NN4 ....68 A5
ay Dr *NHTNW* NN5 ....38 A5
ORO NN8 ....15 E3
g La *NHTNW* NN5 ....49 G4
urne La *NHTNW* NN5 ....49 G4
urne Rd *NHTNW* NN5 ....50 B4
urne St *NHTN* NN1 ....3 K2
urne Wk *NHTN* NN1 ....3 J2
ry La *NHTNE/MOU* NN3 ..41 H4
ry Pl *NHTNE/MOU* NN3 ..41 G4
ster Cl *NHTNS* NN4 ....68 A1
n Cl *NHTNS* NN4 ....68 A1
vay Rd *RSHD/HF* NN10 ....54 A1
se Av *NHTNS* NN4 ....50 A5
am Cl *NHTNE/MOU* NN3 ..53 F1
Rd North *WBORO* NN8 ..16 B4
e St *NHTN* NN1 ....3 G2
rial Sq *NHTN* NN1 ....2 C3
p Rd *NHTNW* NN5 ....49 H2
Wy *NHTNW* NN5 ....49 H2
s Rw *NHTN* NN1 ....3 G2
Gdns *NHTNE/MOU* NN3 ..41 G4
ry Dr *NHTNS* NN4 ....62 A5
Ct *NHTNS* NN4 ....60 D5
ry Rd *NHTNS* NN4 ....64 B3
ields *IR/RAU/FIN* NN9 ....9 F4
Pk *NHTNS* NN4 ....60 D5
v *NHTNS* NN4 ....60 C3
Gv *NHTNS* NN4 ....60 D5
dale Sq *NHTNE/MOU* NN3 ..41 G1
HI *NHTNS* NN4 ....60 A3
Cl *NHTNS* NN4 ....60 C3

Mershe Cl *NHTNS* NN4 ....68 D1
Merthyr Rd *NHTNW* NN5 ....50 C2
Meshaw Crs *NHTNE/MOU* NN3 ..52 B5
The Mews *NHTNS* NN4 ....50 D2
Micklewell La *NHTNE/MOU* NN3 ..41 F1
Middle Grass *IR/RAU/FIN* NN9 ....9 E5
Middle Greeve *NHTNS* NN4 ..69 E2
Middlemarch
NHTNE/MOU NN3 ....41 H3
Middlemead Ct
NHTNE/MOU NN3 ....53 C1
Middlemore *NHTNE/MOU* NN3 ..41 F1
Middle St *RNHPTN* NN7 ....56 C2
Middleton *IR/RAU/FIN* NN9 ....39 E2
Middlewell Ct *NHTNE/MOU* NN3 ..53 F1
Midfield Ct *NHTNE/MOU* NN3 ..41 E2
Midland Rd *IR/RAU/FIN* NN9 ..10 C1
RSHD/HF NN10 ....33 E1
WBORO NN8 ....16 B5
Midshires Wy *BRIX/LBKBY* NN6 ..21 H2
RNHPTN NN7 ....56 C1
RNHPTN NN7 ....71 E4
RNHPTN NN7 ....75 G2
Milbury *BRIX/LBKBY* NN6 ....44 B4
Miles Cl *IR/RAU/FIN* NN9 ....10 D3
Miles Well Ct
NHTNS NN4 ....40 D4
Military Rd *NHTN* NN1 ....51 F3
Militia Cl *NHTNS* NN4 ....68 C1
Millbank *NHTNE/MOU* NN3 ..42 B5
Millbrook Cl *NHTNW* NN5 ....60 C1
Mill Cl *IR/RAU/FIN* NN9 ....11 E2
Miller Hl *NHTNS* NN4 ....60 A3
Miller's Cl *RNHPTN* NN7 ....58 B3
RSHD/HF NN10 ....32 D2
Millers La *NHTN/BOU* NN2 ....38 D5
Millers Cl *WBORO* NN8 ....29 H4
Millers Pk *WBORO* NN8 ....30 A4
Miller St *IR/RAU/FIN* NN9 ....11 E4
Millers Wy *NHTNS* NN4 ....68 D5
Mill Est *RSHD/HF* NN10 ....33 F5
Mill Flds *RSHD/HF* NN10 ....19 F2
Mill La *NHTN/BOU* NN2 ....38 D5
NHTNS NN4 ....61 E4
RNHPTN NN7 ....55 E3
RNHPTN NN7 ....58 B2
Mill Meadow *NHTN/BOU* NN2 ..39 F2
Mill Rd *NHTN* NN1 ....51 E3
WBORO NN8 ....16 C4
WBORO NN8 ....17 G2
Mills Cl *BRIX/LBKBY* NN6 ....44 B3
Millside Cl *NHTNE/MOU* NN3 ..39 F2
Millstone Cl *NHTNW* NN5 ....60 C1
Millway *NHTNW* NN5 ....49 G4
Milner Rd *IR/RAU/FIN* NN9 ....7 H2
Milton Av *WBORO* NN8 ....29 E1
Milton Br *NHTNS* NN4 ....69 E2
Milton Ct *RNHPTN* NN7 ....67 E5
Milton Rd *RNHPTN* NN7 ....70 C1
WBORO NN8 ....30 C5
Milton St North
NHTN/BOU NN2 ....39 G5
Milverton Crs *NHTNE/MOU* NN3 ..52 C5
Mimosa Cl *NHTNE/MOU* NN3 ..52 C2
Minerva Wy *WBORO* NN8 ....15 F4
Mitchell Cl *NHTNW* NN5 ....37 H5
Moat Pl *NHTN* NN1 ....3 G3
Moffatt Ter *WBORO* NN8 ....16 A4
Monarch Rd *NHTN/BOU* NN2 ..51 E1
Monks Hall Rd *NHTN* NN1 ....3 K1
Monks Park Rd *NHTN* NN1 ....51 H5
Monks Pond St *NHTN* NN1 ....2 B2
Monks Rd *BOZ/IR/WOL* NN29 ..46 D2
Monks Wy *WBORO* NN8 ....16 A4
Monmouth Rd *NHTNW* NN5 ..50 C5
Montague Crs *NHTNW* NN5 ..49 G1
Montague St *NHTN* NN1 ....3 G3
Montfort Cl *NHTNW* NN5 ....50 A4
Moores Cl *RNHPTN* NN7 ....57 F5
Moore St *NHTN/BOU* NN2 ....51 H1
Moorfield Sq *NHTNE/MOU* NN3 ..41 G1
Moorland Cl *NHTNE/MOU* NN3 ..41 E4
Moorlands *WBORO* NN8 ....15 F3
Moor Rd *RSHD/HF* NN10 ....19 H5
Mordaunt La *NHTNW* NN5 ..49 H1
Moreton Av *WBORO* NN8 ....29 F2
Moreton Rd *NHTN/BOU* NN2 ..39 E2
Morgan Cl *NHTNW* NN5 ....42 A3
Morgan Dr *BRIX/LBKBY* NN6 ....5 E3
Morris Av *RSHD/HF* NN10 ....19 G5
Morris Cl *WBORO* NN8 ....14 C5
Morris Rd *IR/RAU/FIN* NN9 ....39 F4
Mortar Pit Rd *NHTNE/MOU* NN3 ..42 A1
Mortimer Cl *NHTNS* NN4 ....60 C5
Mortons Bush *NHTNS* NN4 ..68 A2
Motspur Dr *NHTN/BOU* NN2 ..50 D1
Moulton La *NHTNE/MOU* NN3 ..23 F4
Moulton Rd *BRIX/LBKBY* NN6 ..23 F1
Moulton Wy North
NHTNE/MOU NN3 ....40 C1
Moulton Wy South
NHTNE/MOU NN3 ....40 C1
Mountbatten Wy
IR/RAU/FIN NN9 ....11 G2
Mountcastr Ct *NHTNE/MOU* NN3 ..52 E2
Mountfield Rd *IR/RAU/FIN* NN9 ....9 F3
NHTNE/MOU NN3 ....40 A4
Mount Pleasant
BRIX/LBKBY NN6 ....44 B3
Mounts Ct *NHTNE/MOU* NN3 ..41 F1
Muirfield Rd *WBORO* NN8 ....15 E2
Mulberry Cl *NHTNW* NN5 ....50 B3
NHTNS NN4 ....15 G4
The Mullions *NHTNS* NN4 ..68 C3
Mullo Rd *IR/RAU/FIN* NN9 ....8 A2
Mumford Dr *RNHPTN* NN7 ..66 A1
Muncaster Gdns *NHTNS* NN4 ..68 B1
Murray Av *NHTNS* NN4 ....51 F1
Muscott La *NHTNW* NN5 ....49 G4
Muscott St *NHTNW* NN5 ....50 C5
Museum Wy *NHTNS* NN4 ..53 E4
Musgrave Cl *NHTNS* NN4 ..68 D1

Mushroom Field Rd
NHTNS NN3 ....42 B5
Musson Cl *IR/RAU/FIN* NN9 ....9 E4

N

Naomi Cl *NHTNE/MOU* NN3 ..53 F1
Napier Cl *WBORO* NN8 ....28 C1
Naseby Cl *WBORO* NN8 ....54 C5
Naseby St *NHTN/BOU* NN2 ..50 D2
Navigation Rw *NHTN* NN1 ....2 E6
Neale Cl *BOZ/IR/WOL* NN29 ..46 C2
NHTNS NN3 ....52 D2
Near Side *NHTNS* NN4 ....50 B4
Needham Rd *IR/RAU/FIN* NN9 ..11 G4
Nelson St *NHTN* NN1 ....51 E3
Nene Cl *IR/RAU/FIN* NN9 ....11 F1
WBORO NN8 ....15 E3
Nene Dr *NHTNW* NN5 ....38 B5
Nene Pl *NHTNW* NN5 ....38 B5
Nene Ri *RNHPTN* NN7 ....54 D4
Nene Rd *RSHD/HF* NN10 ....19 F4
Nene Valley Wy
NHTNS NN3 ....52 D5
NHTNS NN4 ....61 G4
Nene Vw *IR/RAU/FIN* NN9 ....9 F4
Nene Wk *NHTNW* NN5 ....38 B5
Nene Wy *IR/RAU/FIN* NN9 ....9 F5
NHTNW NN5 ....2 A7
NHTNW NN5 ....58 C1
NHTNW NN5 ....58 D1
RNHPTN NN7 ....55 E3
RNHPTN NN7 ....57 F2
Nesbitt Cl *NHTNE/MOU* NN3 ..53 E5
Nest Farm Crs *WBORO* NN8 ..16 A2
Nest Farm Rd *WBORO* NN8 ..16 A1
Nest La *WBORO* NN8 ....16 B3
Nether Jackson Ct
NHTNE/MOU NN3 ....41 H3
Nethermead Ct
NHTNE/MOU NN3 ....41 F3
Nettle Gap Cl *NHTNS* NN4 ..68 D2
Newbridge La *IR/RAU/FIN* NN9 ..10 C5
Newbury Ct *NHTNS* NN4 ....33 H1
Newcombe Rd *NHTNW* NN5 ..50 C3
Newcomen Rd *WBORO* NN8 ..16 B4
Newington Rd
NHTN/BOU NN2 ....39 E3
Newland Cl *NHTN* NN1 ....2 D2
Newlands *BRIX/LBKBY* NN6 ....4 D4
Newland Wk *NHTN* NN1 ....2 D3
Newman St *RSHD/HF* NN10 ..19 G2
Newnham Rd
NHTN/BOU NN2 ....39 F4
Newport Pagnell Rd
NHTNS NN4 ....68 D1
Newport Pagnell Rd West
NHTNS NN4 ....61 F5
Newport Rd *NHTNW* NN5 ....50 C3
New Rd *NHTNS* NN4 ....68 C1
New South Bridge Rd
NHTNS NN4 ....2 D7
Newstead Cl *NHTNS* NN4 ..42 A4
Newstone Crs *NHTNS* NN4 ..60 A1
New St *BOZ/IR/WOL* NN29 ..31 H4
BRIX/LBKBY NN6 ....4 C4
BRIX/LBKBY NN6 ....44 B5
IR/RAU/FIN NN9 ....11 F1
WBORO NN8 ....16 A4
Newton Cl *RSHD/HF* NN10 ..33 H3
WBORO NN8 ....14 D3
Newton Rd *BOZ/IR/WOL* NN29 ..46 D5
NHTNW NN5 ....49 H2
RSHD/HF NN10 ....19 G4
Newton Road Rbt
NHTNS NN4 ....33 H3
Newton Wd *IR/RAU/FIN* NN9 ..11 C5
New Town Rd *NHTN* NN1 ....2 D6
Newtown Rd *WBORO* NN8 ....30 C3
Nicholas La *IR/RAU/FIN* NN9 ....9 E5
Nicholas Wy *RSHD/HF* NN10 ..32 D1
Nicholls Ct *NHTNE/MOU* NN3 ..41 G2
Nichols Wy *IR/RAU/FIN* NN9 ..11 E1
Nielson Rd *WBORO* NN8 ....16 C1
Nightingale La *WBORO* NN8 ..16 B2
Niort Wy *WBORO* NN8 ....15 E2
Nippendale *RSHD/HF* NN10 ..33 G2
Noble Av *IR/RAU/FIN* NN9 ..11 E4
Norfolk St *NHTN/BOU* NN2 ..51 E2
Norfolk Ter *NHTN/BOU* NN2 ..51 E2
Norman-D-Gate *NHTN* NN1 ....3 H5
Norman Rd *NHTN/BOU* NN2 ..51 B1
Norman Wy *BOZ/IR/WOL* NN29 ..31 H4
WBORO NN8 ....29 F1
Normead Sq *NHTNE/MOU* NN3 ..42 B5
Norris Wy *RSHD/HF* NN10 ..32 C1
Northampton La North
NHTNS NN3 ....24 C4
Northampton La South
NHTNE/MOU NN3 ....53 G1
Northampton Rd
BRIX/LBKBY NN6 ....4 D5
BRIX/LBKBY NN6 ....22 A3
BRIX/LBKBY NN6 ....25 E3
RNHPTN NN7 ....48 A5
RNHPTN NN7 ....65 G5
RNHPTN NN7 ....71 F2
RSHD/HF NN10 ....32 A1
RSHD/HF NN10 ....33 F5
Northcote St *NHTN/BOU* NN2 ..51 E3
North End *RSHD/HF* NN10 ..19 F3
Northen Wy *WBORO* NN8 ....15 H1
Northfield Rd *NHTN/BOU* NN2 ..49 F1
Northfield Wy
NHTN/BOU NN2 ....38 D3
North Hayes Ct
NHTNS NN3 ....41 F2
North Holme Ct
NHTNS NN3 ....40 D2
North Leys Ct
NHTNE/MOU NN3 ....24 C5

North Ov *NHTNW* NN5 ....38 B5
North Paddock Ct
NHTNE/MOU NN3 ....41 F3
North Portway Cl
NHTNS NN3 ....25 F5
North Priors Ct
BRIX/LBKBY NN6 ....44 A2
North Rd *BRIX/LBKBY* NN6 ..39 H1
North St *BRIX/LBKBY* NN6 ..27 F2
IR/RAU/FIN NN9 ....11 G1
RNHPTN NN7 ....60 D5
RSHD/HF NN10 ....33 F1
WBORO NN8 ....15 H4
Northumbria Gdns
NHTNS NN3 ....52 B1
North Western Av
NHTN/BOU NN2 ....38 C3
Northwood Rd
NHTNS NN3 ....40 B5
Norton Rd *NHTNE/MOU* NN3 ..39 E4
Notre Dame Ms *NHTN* NN1 ....3 F3
Nunn Mills Rd *NHTN* NN1 ....3 J5
The Nurseries *NHTN* NN1 ....3 J5
Nursery La *RNHPTN* NN7 ....63 G1
Nursery St *BRIX/LBKBY* NN6 ..27 F2
Nursery Dr *WBORO* NN8 ....16 B1
Nursery Gdns *IR/RAU/FIN* NN9 ..9 E4
Nursery La *NHTN/BOU* NN2 ..39 E4
Nuthall Cl *NHTNE/MOU* NN3 ..53 F2

O

Oak Av *RNHPTN* NN7 ....70 D2
Oak Cl *BOZ/IR/WOL* NN29 ..31 G5
Oakfield *RSHD/HF* NN10 ....19 E5
Oakgrove Pl *NHTNS* NN4 ....68 B2
Oakham Cl *NHTNE/MOU* NN3 ..24 B5
RSHD/HF NN10 ....33 E4
Oaklands *RNHPTN* NN7 ....57 G5
Oaklands Dr *NHTNE/MOU* NN3 ..52 D1
Oakleigh Cl *IR/RAU/FIN* NN9 ..11 E1
Oakleigh Dr *NHTNW* NN5 ....49 G1
Oakley Dr *IR/RAU/FIN* NN9 ..24 D3
Oakley Rd *RSHD/HF* NN10 ..32 D1
Oakley St *NHTN* NN1 ....51 F3
Oakmont Cl *NHTNS* NN4 ....68 A3
Oak Park Cl *NHTNE/MOU* NN3 ..41 G1
Oakpits Wy *RSHD/HF* NN10 ..19 E5
Oaks Dr *RSHD/HF* NN10 ....19 F5
The Oaks *NHTNS* NN4 ....68 D5
Oak St *NHTN* NN1 ....2 E5
RSHD/HF NN10 ....19 F5
Oak Vw *IR/RAU/FIN* NN9 ....6 B5
Oak Wy *IR/RAU/FIN* NN9 ....11 E1
Oakway *WBORO* NN8 ....15 H2
Oakwood Rd *NHTN* NN1 ....51 H1
Oathill Cl *BRIX/LBKBY* NN6 ....4 C5
Oat Hill Dr *NHTNE/MOU* NN3 ..42 B5
Obelisk Cl *NHTN/BOU* NN2 ..23 E5
Obelisk Ri *NHTN/BOU* NN2 ..23 E5
Obelisk Rd *IR/RAU/FIN* NN9 ....8 A1
Octagon Wy *NHTNE/MOU* NN3 ..53 F1
Old Barn Ct *NHTNE/MOU* NN3 ..41 F4
Olde Forde Cl *BRIX/LBKBY* NN6 ....4 D5
Oldenmead Ct
NHTNE/MOU NN3 ....41 F4
Olden Rd *NHTNE/MOU* NN3 ..42 A2
Old Quarry Ct *NHTNE/MOU* NN3 ..41 H3
Old Towcester Rd *NHTNS* NN4 ..2 D7
The Old Vineyard
RSHD/HF NN10 ....19 F5
Oleander Crs *NHTNE/MOU* NN3 ..42 A3
Oliver Cl *RSHD/HF* NN10 ....33 G2
Oliver St *NHTN/BOU* NN2 ..51 G1
Olympia Cl *NHTNS* NN4 ....60 D5
Olympic Wy *WBORO* NN8 ....15 E4
Oransay Cl *NHTNE/MOU* NN3 ..42 A5
Orchard Cl *BOZ/IR/WOL* NN29 ..46 D2
IR/RAU/FIN NN9 ....7 H1
NHTNS NN4 ....68 C2
RNHPTN NN7 ....56 B1
RSHD/HF NN10 ....32 D1
Orchard Gn *NHTNE/MOU* NN3 ..40 C5
Orchard Hl *NHTNE/MOU* NN3 ..53 C1
Orchard La *RNHPTN* NN7 ....65 G3
Orchard Pl *BOZ/IR/WOL* NN29 ..31 G5
Orchard Rd *IR/RAU/FIN* NN9 ....7 H1
IR/RAU/FIN NN9 ....10 D3
The Orchard *RNHPTN* NN7 ..58 B2
Orchard Wy *NHTNW* NN5 ....49 C4
RNHPTN NN7 ....48 A4
RNHPTN NN7 ....58 B1
RNHPTN NN7 ....72 D4
Orient Wy *WBORO* NN8 ....16 A5
Orton Pl *WBORO* NN8 ....15 F2
Orwell Cl *IR/RAU/FIN* NN9 ..11 F1
NHTN/BOU NN2 ....39 F3
Osborn Cl *WBORO* NN8 ....29 G1
Osborne Cl *RSHD/HF* NN10 ..19 H5
Osborne Rd *NHTN/BOU* NN2 ..38 D5
Osler Cl *NHTN/BOU* NN2 ..39 E2
Osmond Dr *NHTNE/MOU* NN3 ..41 G5
Osprey La *NHTN/BOU* NN2 ..16 B2
Osprey Ri *NHTNS* NN4 ....60 D5
Osprey Vw *NHTNE/MOU* NN3 ..60 D5
Oswald Rd *IR/RAU/FIN* NN9 ..11 E4
Osyth Cl *NHTNS* NN4 ....62 B5
Oulton Ri *NHTNE/MOU* NN3 ..41 G5
Oundle Dr *NHTNE/MOU* NN3 ..24 B5
Ouse Cl *NHTN/BOU* NN2 ....39 F4
Outlaw La *WBORO* NN8 ....15 H4
Oval Crs *RSHD/HF* NN10 ..33 H2
Overleys Ct *NHTNE/MOU* NN3 ..41 H2
Overmead Rd *NHTNE/MOU* NN3 ..42 A5
Overslade Cl *NHTNS* NN4 ..60 C5
Overstone La *IR/RAU/FIN* NN9 ..25 E3
Overstone Rd *BRIX/LBKBY* NN6 ..26 B2
NHTN NN1 ....24 C1
NHTNE/MOU NN3 ....24 D3

Owen Cl *WBORO* NN8 ....14 D4
Owen Wy *RSHD/HF* NN10 ..19 E4
Owl Cl *NHTNE/MOU* NN3 ..23 H5
Oxburgh Ct *NHTNS* NN4 ....60 D5
Oxford St *BRIX/LBKBY* NN6 ..44 B4
Oxford St *IR/RAU/FIN* NN9 ....8 B1
NHTNS NN4 ....61 E2
RSHD/HF NN10 ....33 E5
WBORO NN8 ....15 H5
Oxwich Cl *NHTNS* NN4 ....62 A4

P

Paddock La *BRIX/LBKBY* NN6 ..27 F2
Paddock Mill Ct
NHTNE/MOU NN3 ....41 H3
Paddocks Rd *RSHD/HF* NN10 ..32 C1
The Paddocks *BRIX/LBKBY* NN6 ..4 D3
NHTNS NN3 ....57 F5
RNHPTN NN7 ....57 F5
Paddocks Wy *NHTNE/MOU* NN3 ..53 C1
The Paddock *IR/RAU/FIN* NN9 ..11 E4
Padwell Ct *NHTNE/MOU* NN3 ..53 G2
Paget Cl *NHTNS* NN4 ....63 E3
Pagnell Ct *NHTNS* NN4 ....60 E2
Palk Rd *WBORO* NN8 ....16 B5
Palmer Av *IR/RAU/FIN* NN9 ....9 H2
Palmer Cl *WBORO* NN8 ....15 F2
Palmer Sq *NHTNE/MOU* NN3 ..54 A1
Palmerston Rd *NHTN* NN1 ....3 H2
Palm Rd *RSHD/HF* NN10 ....32 C1
Parade Bank *NHTNE/MOU* NN3 ..24 C3
The Parade *NHTN* NN1 ....2 D3
Park Av *IR/RAU/FIN* NN9 ....11 G3
NHTN NN1 ....51 H1
RSHD/HF NN10 ....33 E3
Park Av North *NHTN* NN1 ....52 A1
Park Av South
NHTNE/MOU NN3 ....52 B2
Park Cl *BRIX/LBKBY* NN6 ....26 B2
BRIX/LBKBY NN6 ....45 H5
NHTNW NN5 ....49 E1
RNHPTN NN7 ....58 B2
Park Crs *WBORO* NN8 ....16 A4
Park Crs East *NHTNW* NN5 ..58 B5
Park Crs West *NHTNW* NN5 ..50 B1
Park Dr *NHTNW* NN5 ....50 B1
Parkers Ter *IR/RAU/FIN* NN9 ..7 H2
Park Farm Wy *WBORO* NN8 ..14 D5
Parkfield Av *NHTNS* NN4 ....61 E4
Parkfield Crs *NHTNS* NN4 ..61 E3
Parkfield Rd *NHTNE/MOU* NN3 ..40 D4
Parklands *BRIX/LBKBY* NN6 ..26 B3
NHTNS NN3 ....10 B5
Parklands Av *NHTNE/MOU* NN3 ..40 A2
Parklands Crs *NHTNE/MOU* NN3 ..40 A2
Park La *BRIX/LBKBY* NN6 ....16 A4
NHTNW NN5 ....49 E1
RNHPTN NN7 ....24 A4
RNHPTN NN7 ....70 A1
Park Ms *NHTNS* NN4 ....16 A4
Park Pl *RSHD/HF* NN10 ....33 F2
Park Rd *IR/RAU/FIN* NN9 ....9 E5
IR/RAU/FIN NN9 ....11 G2
RSHD/HF NN10 ....16 A5
WBORO NN8 ....16 A5
Parkside *NHTNE/MOU* NN3 ..42 B5
Park St *BOZ/IR/WOL* NN29 ..47 E3
BRIX/LBKBY NN6 ....45 H3
IR/RAU/FIN NN9 ....11 G2
Park Vw *BRIX/LBKBY* NN6 ..25 E4
Parkway *NHTNE/MOU* NN3 ..52 D2
Parkwood St *NHTNW* NN5 ....2 A3
Parracombe Wy
NHTNE/MOU NN3 ....52 B3
Parsons Cl *NHTNS* NN4 ....42 D3
Parsons Meade *NHTNS* NN4 ..60 A3
Parsons Rd *BOZ/IR/WOL* NN29 ..31 H4
Partridge Cl *NHTN/BOU* NN2 ..38 C2
Parva Cl *NHTNE/MOU* NN3 ..41 E4
Pasteur Cl *NHTN/BOU* NN2 ..38 D2
The Pastures *IR/RAU/FIN* NN9 ..6 A5
NHTN/BOU NN2 ....38 C3
Paterson Rd *WBORO* NN8 ....15 E3
Patterson Cl *NHTNE/MOU* NN3 ..53 E1
Pavilion Dr *NHTNS* NN4 ....61 H4
Paxford Cl *WBORO* NN8 ....29 G3
Paxton Rd *NHTNE/MOU* NN3 ..53 E1
Peace Cl *NHTNS* NN4 ....60 D2
Pearmain Av *WBORO* NN8 ....15 H2
Pearmain Ct *NHTNE/MOU* NN3 ..41 G5
Pear Tree Cl *NHTNE/MOU* NN3 ..41 G5
Peck Wy *RSHD/HF* NN10 ....19 F5
Pegasus Wy *RSHD/HF* NN10 ..18 C5
Pelham Ct *NHTNE/MOU* NN3 ..40 D3
Pell Ct *NHTNE/MOU* NN3 ....41 E4
Pemberton St *RSHD/HF* NN10 ..33 G2
Pembroke Cl *RSHD/HF* NN10 ..33 G3
Pembroke Crs *NHTNW* NN5 ..50 C2
Pembroke Gdns *NHTNW* NN5 ..50 C2
Pembroke Rd *NHTNW* NN5 ..50 C2
Penarth Rd *NHTNW* NN5 ....50 C1
Pendered Rd *WBORO* NN8 ..30 A3
Pendle Rd *NHTNW* NN5 ....49 G2
Penfold Cl *NHTN/BOU* NN2 * ..38 D3
Penfold Dr *NHTNE/MOU* NN3 ..41 H4
Penfold Gdns
NHTNS NN4 ....42 A4
Penfold La *NHTNE/MOU* NN3 ..41 H4
Peninsular Cl *NHTNS* NN4 ..68 C1
Penistone Rd *NHTNE/MOU* NN3 ..41 E4
Pennard Cl *NHTNS* NN4 ....62 B3
Penn Gdns *NHTNW* NN5 ....67 G1
Pennine Wy *NHTNW* NN5 ....49 G2
Pennycress Pl
NHTNE/MOU NN3 ....54 A1
Penrhyn Rd *NHTNS* NN4 ....60 B3
Penrith Dr *WBORO* NN8 ....15 F3
Penvale Rd *NHTNW* NN5 ....49 H4
Peppercorn Wy *NHTNS* NN4 ..68 B2

Percival Cl NHTNW NN5 ....49 H1
Percy Rd NHTN NN1 ....51 H5
Peregrine Pl NHTNS NN4 ....60 C5
Perkins Rd IR/RAU/FIN NN9 ....18 C1
Perry St NHTN NN1 ....51 H5
Pershore Cl WBORO NN8 ....29 E2
Peters La BRIX/LBKBY NN6 ....5 H5
Pevensey Cl RSHD/HF NN10 ....33 H5
Peverel's Wy NHTNW NN5 ....50 A4
Peveril Cl RSHD/HF NN10 ....19 G5
Peveril Rd NHTNW NN5 ....49 F3
Pheasant Wy NHTHN/BOU NN2 ....38 D2
Philip Wy RSHD/HF NN10 ....19 G2
Phoenix St NHTN NN1 ....2 C3
Piccadilly NHTNS NN4 ....60 B5
The Pickerings
 BRIX/LBKBY NN6 ....13 E1
The Piece RNHPTN NN7 ....54 D4
Pie Cnr BRIX/LBKBY NN6 ....26 B1
Pightles Ter RSHD/HF NN10 ....33 G3
Pike La NHTN NN1 ....2 C7
Pikemead Ct NHTNE/MOU NN5 ....41 H5
Pilgrims La RNHPTN NN7 ....37 F5
Pilgrims Pl NHTN NN1 ....61 E3
Pilgrim Wy WBORO NN8 ....15 H5
Pilton Cl IR/RAU/FIN NN9 ....42 A2
Pindar Ri NHTNE/MOU NN3 ....41 E1
Pindar Rd WBORO NN8 ....29 G2
Pine Av BRIX/LBKBY NN6 ....26 B3
Pine Cl IR/RAU/FIN NN9 ....31 G5
 NHTNS NN4 ....68 C5
Pine Copse Cl NHTNW NN5 ....33 E4
Pine Ct RNHPTN NN7 ....34 C5
Pine Crs BRIX/LBKBY NN6 ....26 B3
Pineham Av NHTNE/MOU NN2 ....39 F1
Pine Rdg NHTNE/MOU NN5 ....25 F5
Pine Trees NHTNE/MOU NN5 ....52 D1
Pinewood Rd NHTNE/MOU NN3 ....40 A4
Pioneer Cl NHTNS NN4 ....68 C1
Piper Cl WBORO NN8 ....15 H1
Pippin Cl IR/RAU/FIN NN9 ....54 C5
Pippin Ct RNHPTN NN7 ....54 C5
 RSHD/HF NN10 ....32 C1
 WBORO NN8 ....15 H5
Pippin La NHTNE/MOU NN3 ....41 G5
Pitsford Rd BRIX/LBKBY NN6 ....24 A2
 NHTNE/MOU NN3 ....24 A2
Pitstone Rd NHTNS NN4 ....60 A2
Pitt St WBORO NN8 ....15 G5
Plantagenet Sq NHTNS NN4 ....60 B3
Pleydell Gdns NHTNS NN4 ....60 D3
Pleydell Rd NHTNS NN4 ....61 E3
Plough La NHTNE/MOU NN4 ....38 C1
Ploughmans Wk
 NHTHN/BOU NN2 ....38 D2
Ploughmans Wy NHTNS NN4 ....60 D5
Plumtree Av WBORO NN8 ....16 A2
Poachers Ct NHTNS NN4 ....68 D5
Poachers Wy NHTHN/BOU NN2 ....38 D2
Poitiers Ct NHTNW NN5 ....48 D1
Pomfret Arms Cl RNHPTN NN7 ....2 C7
Pond Bank RNHPTN NN7 ....71 E3
Ponds Cl IR/RAU/FIN NN9 ....11 F2
Pond Wood Cl
 NHTNE/MOU NN3 ....40 B1
Poole St NHTN NN1 ....2 B1
Pope Rd WBORO NN8 ....29 E1
Popham Cl IR/RAU/FIN NN9 ....11 E1
Poplar Cl BOZ/IR/WOL NN29 ....31 G5
 RSHD/HF NN10 ....33 E4
Poplar Ct NHTNE/MOU NN5 ....40 D2
Poplar Rd IR/RAU/FIN NN9 ....47 E3
Poplars Cl IR/RAU/FIN NN9 ....11 E2
Poplar St WBORO NN8 ....16 A4
Poppy Cl RSHD/HF NN10 ....33 G4
Poppyfield Ct NHTNS NN4 ....61 E5
Poppy Leys BRIX/LBKBY NN6 ....12 D1
Porlock Cl NHTNW NN5 ....50 A2
Portchester Gdns
 NHTNS NN4 ....53 F2
Portland Pl NHTN NN1 ....3 H1
Portland Rd IR/RAU/FIN NN9 ....9 F3
 RSHD/HF NN10 ....19 F5
Port Rd RNHPTN NN7 ....36 D4
Portstone Cl NHTNW NN5 ....37 E5
Portwey Cl BRIX/LBKBY NN6 ....5 H5
Pound La NHTNE/MOU NN3 ....24 B3
 WBORO NN8 ....29 H5
Pound Pl IR/RAU/FIN NN9 ....7 H2
The Pound RNHPTN NN7 ....56 B3
Poyntz La NHTNW NN5 ....50 A2
Pratt Rd RSHD/HF NN10 ....33 G2
Premier Wy IR/RAU/FIN NN9 ....18 A2
Prentice Ct NHTNE/MOU NN3 ....41 G2
Prescott Cl NHTNE/MOU NN5 ....42 A3
Pressland Dr RSHD/HF NN10 ....19 G3
Prestbury Rd NHTNW NN5 ....49 E1
Preston Ct NHTNE/MOU NN3 ....41 E4
Prestwold Wy
 NHTNE/MOU NN3 ....41 H2
Primrose Gdns IR/RAU/FIN NN9 ....11 F3
Primrose Hl IR/RAU/FIN NN9 ....11 F3
Primula Cl NHTN NN1 ....52 C4
Prince of Wales Rw
 NHTNE/MOU NN3 ....24 D3
Princess Cl NHTNE/MOU NN3 ....52 B4
Princess Wy WBORO NN8 ....29 G2
Prince St BRIX/LBKBY NN6 ....44 A2
Princes Wk NHTN NN1 ....2 E5
Priors Cl BOZ/IR/WOL NN29 ....31 G4
Priory Cl NHTN NN1 ....52 D4
Priory Crs RNHPTN NN7 ....72 B4
Priory Rd BOZ/IR/WOL NN29 ....46 C2
 WBORO NN8 ....29 H1
Pritchard Cl NHTNE/MOU NN3 ....41 G1
Probyn Cl NHTNE/MOU NN3 ....41 G1
Promenade WBORO NN8 ....15 G4
Prospect Av BOZ/IR/WOL NN29 ....31 F5
 RSHD/HF NN10 ....19 F5
Prospect Cl BOZ/IR/WOL NN29 ....46 C2
Provence Ct NHTNW NN5 ....48 C1
Purbeck Rd RSHD/HF NN10 ....32 B2
Purser Rd NHTN NN1 ....51 H1

Purvis Rd RSHD/HF NN10 ....33 E2
The Pyghtles
 BOZ/IR/WOL NN29 ....46 D4
The Pyghtle BRIX/LBKBY NN6 ....44 A2
 WBORO NN8 ....15 H1
Pyghtle Wy NHTNS NN4 ....60 A5
Pyket Wy NHTNE/MOU NN3 ....52 D2
Pyramid Cl NHTNE/MOU NN3 ....41 E5
Pytchley Cl BRIX/LBKBY NN6 ....4 D4
Pytchley Ri WBORO NN8 ....29 F1
Pytchley Rd NHTNE/MOU NN3 ....32 D1
Pytchley St NHTN NN1 ....3 G2
Pytchley Vw NHTNS NN4 ....24 D3
Pytchley Wy BRIX/LBKBY NN6 ....4 D4
 NHTNS NN4 ....37 F5

Q
Quakers Cl RNHPTN NN7 ....57 F5
Quantock Crs NHTNW NN5 ....49 H2
Quarry Park Cl
 NHTNS NN3 ....40 B1
Quarry Rd BRIX/LBKBY NN6 ....5 E3
Quarterstone NHTNW NN4 ....59 H4
Quebec Cl NHTNS NN4 ....68 C1
Queen Eleanor Rd NHTNS NN4 ....60 D3
Queen Eleanor Ter NHTNS NN4 ....61 E5
Queens Crs NHTHN/BOU NN2 ....39 F5
Queensland Gdns
 NHTHN/BOU NN2 ....39 E5
Queens Rd BOZ/IR/WOL NN29 ....46 D3
 NHTN NN1 ....3 G1
Queen St BRIX/LBKBY NN6 ....44 A2
 IR/RAU/FIN NN9 ....9 E4
 RSHD/HF NN10 ....33 F2
 WBORO NN8 ....15 H5
Queensway RSHD/HF NN10 ....19 G4
 WBORO NN8 ....29 F1
Queenswood Av
 NHTNS NN3 ....40 D2
Quernstone La NHTNS NN4 ....60 A2
Quinton Rd NHTNS NN4 ....68 D4
Quintonside NHTNS NN4 ....68 D5
Quorn Cl WBORO NN8 ....15 F5
Quorn Rd RSHD/HF NN10 ....32 D1
Quorn Wy NHTN NN1 ....2 B1

R
Radleigh Cl NHTNS NN4 ....60 C5
Radstone Wy NHTHN/BOU NN2 ....39 E2
Raeburn Rd NHTHN/BOU NN2 ....39 H5
Raglan Cl RSHD/HF NN10 ....33 H5
Raglan St NHTN NN1 ....3 G2
Rainsborough Crs NHTNS NN4 ....60 B1
Raisins Field Cl
 NHTNS NN4 ....42 A4
Rakestone Cl NHTNS NN4 ....68 B2
Ramsay Cl IR/RAU/FIN NN9 ....11 E1
Randall Rd NHTHN/BOU NN2 ....39 G5
Rands Wy IR/RAU/FIN NN9 ....11 G3
Ranelagh Rd WBORO NN8 ....16 B4
Ransome Rd NHTNS NN4 ....61 F2
Raunds Rd IR/RAU/FIN NN9 ....10 C4
Ravensbank RSHD/HF NN10 ....19 F4
Ravens Cft NHTNS NN4 ....68 D5
Ravens Wy NHTNE/MOU NN5 ....54 A2
Rawley Crs NHTNW NN5 ....49 E1
Raymond Cl BOZ/IR/WOL NN29 ....47 E4
Raymond Rd NHTNW NN5 ....50 B1
Raysford Rd NHTNW NN5 ....50 B1
Rea Cl NHTNS NN4 ....68 A1
Rectory Cl IR/RAU/FIN NN9 ....10 B4
Rectory Farm Rd
 NHTNE/MOU NN3 ....42 A2
Rectory La RNHPTN NN7 ....67 E5
Rectory Rd RSHD/HF NN10 ....33 F1
Redding Cl RSHD/HF NN10 ....33 E5
Red Hill Crs BOZ/IR/WOL NN29 ....46 D2
Redhill Wy IR/RAU/FIN NN9 ....15 G1
Red House Rd
 NHTNS NN4 ....23 H5
Redland Dr NHTHN/BOU NN2 ....38 C3
Redruth Cl NHTNS NN4 ....60 D4
Redwell Rd WBORO NN8 ....15 H5
Redwing Av NHTNE/MOU NN3 * 24 C5
Redwood Cl BOZ/IR/WOL NN29 ....46 C2
Reedham Cl NHTNW NN5 ....49 G1
Reedhill NHTNS NN4 ....50 A3
Reedway NHTNE/MOU NN3 ....40 A3
Regal Cl NHTNE/MOU NN3 ....39 H1
Regal Ct RSHD/HF NN10 ....33 G3
Regents Ga NHTNS NN4 ....68 C5
Regent St IR/RAU/FIN NN9 ....7 G2
 NHTN NN1 ....2 E4
 WBORO NN8 ....16 A4
Regiment Cl NHTNS NN4 ....68 C1
Reims Ct NHTN NN1 ....37 E5
Rennishaw Wy
 NHTNE/MOU NN3 ....39 H4
Repton Ct RNHPTN NN7 ....40 D3
Resthaven Rd NHTNS NN4 ....68 B3
Restormel Cl RSHD/HF NN10 ....33 H5
Retford Ct NHTNE/MOU NN3 ....41 F5
Reynard Wy NHTHN/BOU NN2 ....39 E2
Reynolds Cl WBORO NN8 ....15 H2
Rhosili Rd NHTNS NN4 ....62 A3
Ribble Cl NHTN NN1 ....38 B5
 NHTNS NN4 ....62 A3
Richardson Wy IR/RAU/FIN NN9 ....11 G1
Richmond Cl RSHD/HF NN10 ....33 G4
Richmond Ter NHTNW NN5 ....2 A1
Rickyard Rd NHTNS NN4 ....40 D4
The Ridge BOZ/IR/WOL NN29 ....29 G5
Ridgeway NHTNE/MOU NN3 ....52 C2
 WBORO NN8 ....15 H2

The Ridings BRIX/LBKBY NN6 ....5 E4
 NHTN NN1 ....2 E5
 RNHPTN NN7 ....72 C4
Riley Cl NHTNE/MOU NN3 ....42 A2
Rillwood Ct NHTNE/MOU NN5 ....41 E5
Ring Wy NHTNS NN4 ....60 C2
Ringwell Cl IR/RAU/FIN NN9 ....9 E3
Ringwood Cl NHTHN/BOU NN2 ....38 C2
Ripon Cl NHTNS NN4 ....60 C3
The Rise NHTHN/BOU NN2 ....38 D4
Riverside Ct RNHPTN NN7 ....58 B1
Riverside Wy NHTN NN1 ....3 J5
Riverstone Wy NHTNS NN4 ....59 H4
Riverwell NHTNE/MOU NN3 ....42 B5
Rixon Cl NHTNE/MOU NN3 ....53 F1
Rixon Rd WBORO NN8 ....16 C2
Roberts St RSHD/HF NN10 ....33 G2
 WBORO NN8 ....15 G5
Robert St NHTN NN1 ....2 E1
Robinia Cl NHTNS NN4 ....60 A2
Robin La WBORO NN8 ....16 A2
Robinson Rd RSHD/HF NN10 ....33 G2
Rochelle Wy NHTNS NN5 ....37 E5
Roche Wy WBORO NN8 ....15 H5
Rockcroft NHTNS NN4 ....68 B2
Rockingham Ct NHTNE/MOU NN3 ....53 E4
Rockingham Rd NHTNS NN4 ....61 E3
Rockleigh Cl IR/RAU/FIN NN9 ....8 A1
Rock Rd NHTN NN1 ....8 A1
Rock St WBORO NN8 ....15 H4
Roe Rd NHTN NN1 ....51 H2
Roland Wy RSHD/HF NN10 ....19 E3
Rolfe Crs RNHPTN NN7 ....56 B5
Roman Cl NHTNS NN4 ....68 D3
Roman Wy BOZ/IR/WOL NN29 ....31 H5
Romany Rd NHTNE/MOU NN2 ....39 G5
Rookery La NHTNE/MOU NN2 ....38 C2
Rose Av RSHD/HF NN10 ....32 D3
Rosebery Av NHTNW NN5 ....50 B4
Rose Cl BOZ/IR/WOL NN29 ....46 C2
Rosedale Rd NHTNE/MOU NN3 ....42 A5
Rose Field Sq
 NHTNS NN3 ....42 A5
Rose Hl IR/RAU/FIN NN9 ....7 H1
Roseholm Cl NHTNS NN4 ....52 B4
Rosemoor Dr NHTNS NN4 ....68 A1
Rosenella Cl NHTNS NN4 ....60 B2
Rosette Cl NHTNW NN5 ....49 G2
Rosgill Pl NHTNE/MOU NN3 ....40 B5
Ross Rd NHTNW NN5 ....50 A4
Rotherhithe Cl NHTNS NN4 ....60 D5
Rothersthorpe Av NHTNS NN4 ....60 C5
Rothersthorpe Crs NHTNS NN4 ....60 C2
Rothersthorpe Rd NHTNS NN4 ....16 C2
Rothesay Rd NHTHN/BOU NN2 ....39 H5
Rothesay Ter NHTHN/BOU NN2 ....39 G5
Rotten Rw BOZ/IR/WOL NN29 ....46 C3
Rotton Rw IR/RAU/FIN NN9 ....11 F1
Rowan Cl NHTNE/MOU NN3 ....40 C2
Rowan Ct WBORO NN8 ....15 G4
Rowlandson Cl
 NHTNE/MOU NN3 ....53 E1
Rowley Wy NHTNE/MOU NN3 ....39 G1
Rowtree Rd NHTNS NN4 ....67 G1
Roxeby Wk NHTNW NN5 ....49 H1
Ruddington Cl
 NHTNS NN4 ....53 E5
Rudge Ms NHTNW NN5 ....48 D2
Rufford Av NHTNE/MOU NN3 ....53 E3
Rugby Wy IR/RAU/FIN NN9 ....9 F4
Rushmere Av NHTN NN1 ....52 B4
Rushmere Crs NHTN NN1 ....52 B5
Rushmere Rd NHTN NN1 ....52 B5
Rushmere Wy NHTN NN1 ....52 B4
Rushmills NHTNS NN4 ....19 E5
Rushy End NHTNS NN4 ....67 H2
Ruskin Av WBORO NN8 ....15 G5
Ruskin Rd NHTHN/BOU NN2 ....39 E5
Russell Sq NHTHN/MOU NN3 ....40 C1
Russell Wy RSHD/HF NN10 ....19 G3
Russet Dr NHTNE/MOU NN3 ....41 G5
Rutherford Dr WBORO NN8 ....14 C4
Rutland Wk NHTNE/MOU NN3 ....24 B5
Rycroft Cl WBORO NN8 ....15 F4
Rydalside NHTNS NN4 ....60 B2
Rydal Av NHTNE/MOU NN3 ....52 B4
Ryeburn Wy WBORO NN8 ....15 G4
Ryebury Hl WBORO NN8 ....7 G4
Rye Cl RSHD/HF NN10 ....33 G4
Ryehill Cl NHTNE/MOU NN3 ....18 C1
Ryeholme Br
 BOZ/IR/WOL NN29 ....45 G4
Ryeland Cl NHTNS NN4 ....49 E1
Ryeland Wy NHTNW NN5 ....48 D2
Ryland Rd NHTNE/MOU NN3 ....24 C4
 NHTHN/BOU NN2 ....39 G5
Ryle Dr WBORO NN8 ....14 C5
Ryngwell Cl BRIX/LBKBY NN6 ....4 D5

S
Sackville St IR/RAU/FIN NN9 ....11 F2
Saddleback Rd NHTNW NN5 ....49 H4
Saddlers Sq NHTNE/MOU NN3 ....41 F1
The Saddlers NHTNS NN4 ....68 D5
Saddlers Wy IR/RAU/FIN NN9 ....10 D5
Saffron Cl NHTN NN1 ....68 B3
Saffron Rd RSHD/HF NN10 ....33 E3
Sage Cl NHTNE/MOU NN3 ....41 E3
St Alban's Cl NHTNE/MOU NN3 ....40 B4
St Albans Pl BOZ/IR/WOL NN29 ....46 C4
St Alban's Rd
 NHTNS NN3 ....40 B4
St Andrews Crs WBORO NN8 ....29 G3
St Andrew's Rd NHTN NN1 ....2 B5
St Andrew's St NHTN NN1 ....2 C1

St Barnabas St WBORO NN8 ....15 G5
St Benedicts Mt NHTNS NN4 ....60 A3
St Crispin Av WBORO NN8 ....29 H2
St Crispin Crs NHTNW NN5 ....48 D2
St Crispin Development
 RNHPTN NN7 ....48 D3
St Crispin Rd BRIX/LBKBY NN6 ....44 B5
St Davids Cl BRIX/LBKBY NN6 ....4 D5
St David's Rd BRIX/LBKBY NN6 ....4 C4
 NHTNE/MOU NN2 ....39 F5
 RSHD/HF NN10 ....32 E1
St Dunstans Rd NHTNS NN4 ....60 A4
St Edmund's Rd NHTN NN1 ....3 G3
St Edmund's St NHTN NN1 ....3 H2
St Emilion Cl NHTNW NN5 ....48 D1
St Francis Av NHTNW NN5 ....50 C2
St George's Av
 NHTHN/BOU NN2 ....51 F2
St George's St NHTN NN1 ....2 D5
St George's Wy RSHD/HF NN10 ....32 D1
St Giles' Sq NHTN NN1 ....2 E4
St Giles' St NHTN NN1 ....2 E4
St Giles' Ter NHTN NN1 ....3 F3
St Gregory's Rd
 NHTNS NN3 ....40 D4
St James' Cl RSHD/HF NN10 ....19 F5
St James Mill Rd NHTNE/MOU NN5 ....2 A6
St James Mill Rd East
 NHTNW NN5 ....2 A7
St James' Park Rd NHTNW NN5 ....50 C4
St James' Rd NHTNW NN5 ....50 C4
St James' St NHTN NN1 ....2 D5
St John's Av NHTNE/MOU NN2 ....39 E1
St Johns Cl RNHPTN NN7 ....66 A2
St John's St NHTN NN1 ....2 D5
 NHTNS NN4 ....18 H5
St John's Ter NHTN NN1 ....2 E5
St Julien Cl NHTNW NN5 ....50 C2
St Katharine's Av
 BOZ/IR/WOL NN29 ....31 G3
St Katherines Ct NHTN NN1 * 2 B5
St Katherines Cl NHTNS NN4 ....2 C3
St Laurence Wy
 IR/RAU/FIN NN9 ....10 B4
St Leonards Ct NHTNS NN4 ....61 E2
St Leonard's Rd NHTNS NN4 ....61 E2
St Lukes Cl NHTNW NN5 ....48 D2
St Margarets Av
 RSHD/HF NN10 ....33 E3
St Mark's Cl RSHD/HF NN10 ....32 C2
St Martins Cl NHTHN/BOU NN2 ....48 D3
St Mary's Av RSHD/HF NN10 ....33 E3
St Marys Ct NHTN NN1 ....2 C4
 RNHPTN NN7 ....70 B1
St Marys Rd BOZ/IR/WOL NN29 ....46 D3
St Mary's St NHTN NN1 ....2 C3
St Michael's Av NHTN NN1 ....3 G2
St Michael's La
 BOZ/IR/WOL NN29 ....46 D5
St Michael's Mt NHTNS NN4 ....51 G5
St Michael's Rd NHTN NN1 ....3 F2
St Nicholas Rd
 BOZ/IR/WOL NN29 ....45 F1
St Patrick St NHTN NN1 ....2 C1
St Paul's Rd NHTHN/BOU NN2 ....51 G2
St Peter's Av RSHD/HF NN10 ....32 D2
St Peter's Br NHTN NN1 ....2 C4
St Peter's Gdns
 NHTNE/MOU NN3 ....52 D1
St Peters Sq NHTN NN1 ....2 D4
St Peter's Sq IR/RAU/FIN NN9 ....9 F4
St Peters Wk NHTN NN1 ....2 C4
St Peter's Wy NHTN NN1 ....2 B4
 RNHPTN NN7 ....54 D3
St Rochus Dr WBORO NN8 ....30 A3
St Thomas Rd RNHPTN NN7 ....54 B2
Salcey St NHTN NN1 ....61 E3
Salem La WBORO NN8 ....15 H4
Salisbury Rd WBORO NN8 ....50 H2
Salisbury St NHTHN/BOU NN2 ....50 D2
Sallow Av NHTNE/MOU NN3 ....42 A4
Salthouse Rd NHTN NN1 ....62 A3
Salt Pikes BRIX/LBKBY NN6 ....12 D1
Saltwell Sq NHTNE/MOU NN3 ....42 A4
Samwell Wy NHTNS NN4 ....59 G4
Sanders Cl WBORO NN8 ....6 D5
Sanders Rd WBORO NN8 ....29 E1
Sandfield Cl NHTNE/MOU NN3 ....40 B1
Sandhill Rd NHTNW NN5 ....50 C4
Sandhills Cl NHTHN/BOU NN2 ....38 D1
Sandhills Rd NHTHN/BOU NN2 ....38 D1
Sandhurst Cl NHTNS NN4 ....60 D5
Sandiland Rd
 NHTNE/MOU NN3 ....40 B5
Sandover NHTNS NN4 ....68 B2
Sandpiper La WBORO NN8 ....16 A2
Sandringham Cl NHTN NN1 ....52 B5
 WBORO NN8 ....29 F2
Sandringham Rd NHTN NN1 ....52 A3
Sandy Cl WBORO NN8 ....15 H3
Sandy Hill La
 NHTNE/MOU NN3 ....25 E3
Sandy La BRIX/LBKBY NN6 ....21 G4
 NHTNW NN5 ....48 D1
Saneco La BRIX/LBKBY NN6 ....4 D5
Sansom Ct NHTNE/MOU NN3 ....52 B4
Sarek Pk NHTN NN1 ....60 B5
Sargeants La NHTNS NN4 ....68 A4
Sartoris Rd RSHD/HF NN10 ....32 D2
Saruman La NHTNE/MOU NN3 ....41 H2
Sassoon Cl WBORO NN8 ....14 D4
Savill Cl NHTNS NN4 ....68 B3
Saxby Crs WBORO NN8 ....16 C5
Saxon Av NHTNS NN4 ....68 C4
Saxon Rd NHTHN/BOU NN2 ....19 F2
Saxon Ri BOZ/IR/WOL NN29 ....32 A4
 BRIX/LBKBY NN6 ....44 A5
Saxon St NHTHN/BOU NN2 ....51 E1
Saxon Wy IR/RAU/FIN NN9 ....11 G2
Scaldwell Rd BRIX/LBKBY NN6 ....5 H3

Scarborough St
 IR/RAU/FIN NN9
Scarletwell St NHTNW NN1
The Scarplands NHTNW NN5
Scharpwell IR/RAU/FIN NN9
Scholars Ct NHTN NN1
School Dr RSHD/HF NN10
School Hl BOZ/IR/WOL NN29
School La BOZ/IR/WOL NN29
 NHTNE/MOU NN3 *
 NHTNS NN4
 RNHPTN NN7
 RSHD/HF NN10
School Rd BOZ/IR/WOL NN29
Scirocco Cl NHTNS NN4
Scotia Cl NHTNS NN4
Scots Mere IR/RAU/FIN NN9
Scott Rd WBORO NN8
Scully Cl NHTNS NN4
Seagrave Ct NHTNE/MOU NN3
Seaton Dr NHTNE/MOU NN5
Second Av WBORO NN8
Second La NHTNW NN5
Sedgewick Ct NHTNE/MOU NN5
Seedfield Cl NHTNE/MOU NN3
Semilong Rd NHTN/BOU NN2
Sentinel Rd NHTNS NN4
Sentry Cl NHTN NN1
Senwick Dr WBORO NN8
Senwick Rd WBORO NN8
Severn Cl WBORO NN8
Severn Dr NHTNW NN5
Seymour St NHTNW NN5
Shadowfax Dr
 NHTNE/MOU NN3
Shakespeare Rd NHTN NN1
 RSHD/HF NN10
 WBORO NN8
Shale End NHTNW NN5
Shannon Cl RSHD/HF NN10
Shap Gn NHTNE/MOU NN3
Shard Cl NHTNS NN4
Sharman Rd NHTNW NN5
 WBORO NN8
Sharrow Pl NHTNE/MOU NN3
Shatterstone NHTNS NN4
Shaw Cl WBORO NN8
Shearf Cl NHTNW NN5
Shearwater La WBORO NN8
Shedfield Wy NHTNS NN4
Sheep St NHTN NN1
Sheerwater Dr
 NHTNE/MOU NN3
Sheffield Ct IR/RAU/FIN NN9
Sheffield Wy BRIX/LBKBY NN6
Sheilds Rd
 BRIX/LBKBY NN6
Shelleycotes Rd
 BRIX/LBKBY NN6
Shelley Dr RSHD/HF NN10
Shelley Rd WBORO NN8
Shelley St NHTHN/BOU NN2
Shelsley Dr NHTNE/MOU NN3
Shelton Rd IR/RAU/FIN NN9
Shepherd Cl NHTHN/BOU NN2
Shepherds Hl
 BOZ/IR/WOL NN29
Shepherds Wk RNHPTN NN7
 RNHPTN NN7
Shepperton Cl
 NHTNE/MOU NN3
Sheraton Cl NHTNE/MOU NN3
Sheriff Rd NHTN NN1
Sherwood Av NHTNE/MOU NN3
Shipton Wy RSHD/HF NN10
Shire Pl NHTNE/MOU NN3
Shirley Rd RSHD/HF NN10
Shoal Creek NHTN NN1
The Shortlands IR/RAU/FIN NN9
Short La RNHPTN NN7
 WBORO NN8
Short Stocks RSHD/HF NN10
Shortwoods Cl IR/RAU/FIN NN9
Shurville Cl BRIX/LBKBY NN6
Sibley Rd IR/RAU/FIN NN9
Siddons Wy NHTNE/MOU NN3
Sidebrook Ct NHTNE/MOU NN3
Sidegate La WBORO NN8
The Sidings IR/RAU/FIN NN9
Silverdale Gv RSHD/HF NN10
Silverdale Rd NHTNE/MOU NN3
Silverstone Cl NHTHN/BOU NN2
Silver St BRIX/LBKBY NN6
 NHTN NN1
 NHTNS NN4
Simons Wk NHTN NN1
Simpson Av RSHD/HF NN10
Sinclair Dr WBORO NN8
Sir John Pascoe Wy
 NHTNS NN4
Siward Vw NHTNW NN5
Skawie Ct NHTNE/MOU NN3
Skelton Wk NHTNE/MOU NN3
Sketty Cl NHTNS NN4
Sketty Rd NHTNE/MOU NN3
Skinner Av NHTNW NN5
Skinner's Hl RSHD/HF NN10
Skipton Cl NHTNS NN4
Sladeswell Ct NHTNE/MOU NN3
Slaters Cl RSHD/HF NN10
The Slips RSHD/HF NN10
The Slip BRIX/LBKBY NN6
Smith Ct NHTNS NN4
Smitherway RNHPTN NN7
Smithfield Pl IR/RAU/FIN NN9
The Smithy NHTNE/MOU NN3
Smyth Ct NHTNE/MOU NN3
Snetterton Cl NHTNE/MOU NN3
Snowbell Sq NHTNE/MOU NN3
Somerford Rd WBORO NN8
Somerset St NHTN NN1
Sorrel Cl NHTNS NN4
Sotheby Ri NHTNE/MOU NN3
Southampton Rd NHTNS NN4

Westminster Rd *WBORO* NN8 ......**15** F2
Westone Av *NHTNE/MOU* NN3 ....**53** E1
Weston Mill La
  NHTNE/MOU NN3 ....**53** E4
Weston Wy *NHTNE/MOU* NN3.......**52** C2
West Ov *NHTNW* NN5 ....**50** B1
West Paddock Ct
  NHTNE/MOU NN3 ....**41** F3
West Priors Ct
  NHTNE/MOU NN3 ....**41** F3
West Rdg *NHTNN/BOU* NN2 ....**39** F4
West Rising *NHTNS* NN4 ....**68** B1
West St *BRIX/LBKBY* NN6 ....**42** D4
  BRIX/LBKBY NN6 ....**43** H3
  IR/RAU/FIN NN9 ....**10** A5
  IR/RAU/FIN NN9 ....**31** F5
  NHTN NN1 ....**3** J2
  NHTNE/MOU NN3 ....**24** B3
  RSHD/HF NN10 ....**33** F2
West Villa Rd *WBORO* NN8 ....**15** H5
West Wy *BRIX/LBKBY* NN6 ....**43** H2
Wetenhall Rd *IR/RAU/FIN* NN9 ....**10** C4
Wetheral Cl *NHTNS* NN4 ....**40** C3
Whaddon Cl *NHTN* NN1 ....**60** A4
Whaddon Fld *BRIX/LBKBY* NN6.......**5** E3
Whalley Gv *RNHPTN* NN7 ....**54** D4
Wharf Rd *RSHD/HF* NN10 ....**19** F4
Wheatcroft Gdns
  NHTNE/MOU NN3 ....**33** F2
Wheatens Ct *BRIX/LBKBY* NN6 .....**13** E1
Wheatfield Gdns
  NHTNE/MOU NN3 ....**52** B1
Wheatfield Rd
  NHTNE/MOU NN3 ....**52** B1
Wheatfield Rd North
  NHTNE/MOU NN3 ....**40** B5
Wheatfield Rd South
  NHTNE/MOU NN3 ....**52** B1
Wheatfield Ter
  NHTNE/MOU NN3 ....**52** B1
Wheelwright Cl
  IR/RAU/FIN NN9 ....**11** C1
Whernside *WBORO* NN8 ....**15** E3
Whernside Wy *NHTNW* NN5 ....**49** C2
Whilton Rd *NHTNN/BOU* NN2 ....**39** F5
  RNHPTN NN7 ....**54** C2
Whistlers Cl *NHTNS* NN4 ....**59** H4

Whiston Rd *NHTNN/BOU* NN2 ......**39** F3
  RNHPTN NN7 ....**55** G4
  RNHPTN NN7 ....**65** F5
The White Cl *RSHD/HF* NN10 ....**19** G5
White Delves *WBORO* NN8 ....**15** G2
White Doe Dr *NHTNE/MOU* NN3 ...**24** C5
Whitefield Rd *NHTNW* NN5 ....**49** F1
Whitefield Wy *IR/RAU/FIN* NN9 ....**11** E1
Whitefriars *RSHD/HF* NN10 ....**32** D3
Whitegates *NHTNS* NN4 ....**59** H4
Whiteheart Cl
  NHTNE/MOU NN3 ....**41** H5
White Hills Crs
  NHTNN/BOU NN2 ....**38** D1
White Hills Wy
  NHTNN/BOU NN2 ....**38** D1
Whiteland Rd *NHTNE/MOU* NN3...**40** C5
Whitesands Wy *NHTNS* NN4 ....**59** G4
Whites Ri *IR/RAU/FIN* NN9 ....**9** E5
White Wy *BRIX/LBKBY* NN6 ....**44** A2
Whitfield Wy *NHTNN/BOU* NN2 ....**39** F2
Whitlock Cl *NHTNE/MOU* NN3 ......**24** C4
Whitsundale Cl *IR/RAU/FIN* NN9 .....**7** H2
Whittam Cl *IR/RAU/FIN* NN9 ....**11** E1
Whittemore Rd *RSHD/HF* NN10 ....**33** H1
Whittlebury Cl
  NHTNE/MOU NN3 ....**39** F2
Whittle Cl *WBORO* NN8 ....**14** D3
Whittles Cross *NHTNS* NN4 ....**69** E2
Whitworth Crs
  BRIX/LBKBY NN6 ....**44** A2
Whitworth Rd *NHTN* NN1 ....**51** H5
  WBORO NN8 ....**16** C4
Whitworth Wy *IR/RAU/FIN* NN9 ...**18** C1
  WBORO NN8 ....**30** B3
Whytewell Rd *WBORO* NN8 ....**15** H5
Wickery Dene *NHTNS* NN4 ....**69** E2
Wilberforce St *NHTN* NN1 ....**3** H2
Wilbye Gra *WBORO* NN8 ....**29** F2
Wilby La *BOZ/IR/WOL* NN29 ....**29** F5
Wilby Rd *BRIX/LBKBY* NN6 ....**27** F3
Wilby St *NHTN* NN1 ....**3** H5
Wilby Wy *WBORO* NN8 ....**29** F3
Wilce Av *WBORO* NN8 ....**30** A3
Wildacre Rd *RSHD/HF* NN10 ....**32** C2
Wildern La *NHTNS* NN4 ....**68** A5
Wilford Av *NHTNE/MOU* NN3 ....**53** F2
Wilkie Rd *WBORO* NN8 ....**15** H1

William Steele Wy
  RSHD/HF NN10 ....**19** G3
William St *IR/RAU/FIN* NN9 ....**8** A2
  NHTN NN1 ....**2** E1
William's Wy *BOZ/IR/WOL* NN29 ..**47** E4
  RSHD/HF NN10 ....**19** F4
William Trigg Cl
  IR/RAU/FIN NN9 ....**18** C1
Williton Cl *NHTNE/MOU* NN3 ....**52** D3
Willow Brook Sq
  NHTNE/MOU NN3 ....**42** A4
Willow Crs *NHTNS* NN4 ....**63** E3
Willow Herb Cl *RSHD/HF* NN10 .....**33** C5
Willow La *NHTNS* NN4 ....**63** E3
Willow Rt *NHTNE/MOU* NN3...........**50** C4
Willow Vw *RNHPTN* NN7 ....**58** A2
Wilson Crs *IR/RAU/FIN* NN9 ....**9** E5
Wilson Rd *NHTNS* NN4 ....**33** E2
Wilson Wy *BRIX/LBKBY* NN6 ....**44** A4
Wimbledon St *NHTNW* NN5............**50** C4
Wimborne Cl *NHTNE/MOU* NN3 ...**42** B4
Winchester Cl *NHTNS* NN4 ....**61** E4
Winchester Rd *NHTNS* NN4 ....**61** E5
  RSHD/HF NN10 ....**32** A2
Windermere Dr *RSHD/HF* NN10 ....**19** F1
  WBORO NN8 ....**15** E4
Windermere Wy
  NHTNE/MOU NN3 ....**40** C3
Windflower Pl
  NHTNE/MOU NN3 ....**42** B5
Windingbrook La *NHTNS* NN4 ....**68** A4
Windmill Av *IR/RAU/FIN* NN9 ....**11** F2
  RNHPTN NN7 ....**71** F4
Windmill Banks *RSHD/HF* NN10 ....**19** F2
Windmill Cl *BOZ/IR/WOL* NN29 .....**47** E5
  WBORO NN8 ....**29** C2
Windmill Gld *BRIX/LBKBY* NN6 ....**4** C5
Windmill Gv *IR/RAU/FIN* NN9 ....**11** F2
Windmill La *IR/RAU/FIN* NN9 ....**11** E1
  RNHPTN NN7 ....**65** F5
Windmill Rd *IR/RAU/FIN* NN9 ....**9** E5
  RSHD/HF NN10 ....**33** E2
Windmill Ter *NHTNN/BOU* NN2 ....**39** F3
Windrush Rd *NHTNS* NN4 ....**61** H5
Windrush Wy *NHTNW* NN5 ....**50** A4
Windsor Crs *NHTNW* NN5 ....**50** A4
Windsor Rd *RSHD/HF* NN10 ....**33** C1
  WBORO NN8 ....**29** H3

Windyridge *NHTNN/BOU* NN2 ......**39** F4
Winnington Cl
  NHTNE/MOU NN3 ....**42** A2
Winsford Wy *NHTNE/MOU* NN3 ...**52** D5
Winstanley Rd *WBORO* NN8 ....**16** B5
Winston Cl *NHTNE/MOU* NN3 ....**40** C2
  RNHPTN NN7 ....**56** B5
Wisley Cl *NHTNS* NN4 ....**68** A1
Wisteria Cl *RSHD/HF* NN10 ....**33** F5
Wisteria Wy *NHTNE/MOU* NN3 .....**52** C4
Witham Gn *NHTNW* NN5 ....**38** A5
Witham Wk *NHTNW* NN5 ....**38** B5
Witham Wy *NHTNW* NN5 ....**50** B1
Witton Rd *NHTNW* NN5 ....**38** C5
Woburn Ga *NHTNE/MOU* NN3 ....**42** B4
Wollaston Rd
  BOZ/IR/WOL NN29 ....**31** F5
Wollaton Gdns
  NHTNE/MOU NN3 ....**53** F2
Wood Avens Cl *NHTNS* NN4 ....**60** A4
Woodcote Av *NHTNE/MOU* NN3 ..**39** H5
Woodford St *NHTN* NN1 ....**3** H5
Woodford Wk *NHTN* NN1 ....**3** H3
Woodgate Rd *NHTNS* NN4 ....**68** D2
Woodhall Cl *NHTNS* NN4 ....**59** H4
Woodhill Rd *NHTN* NN1 ....**2** E4
Woodhill Rd *NHTNW* NN5 ....**49** F1
Woodland Av *BRIX/LBKBY* NN6 .....**25** H3
Woodland Cl *NHTNS* NN4 ....**52** A1
Woodland Ct *NHTNW* NN5 ....**37** F5
Woodland Rd *RSHD/HF* NN10 ....**32** D2
Woodlands Gra
  BRIX/LBKBY NN6 ....**44** C3
Woodlands Rd
  BOZ/IR/WOL NN29 ....**31** G5
Woodland Wk
  NHTNE/MOU NN3 ....**31** H1
Woodley Cha *NHTNW* NN5 ....**49** F1
Woodpecker Wy *NHTNS* NN4 ....**67** F1
Woodrush Wy
  NHTNE/MOU NN3 ....**40** C1
Woodside *BRIX/LBKBY* NN6 ....**26** B3
Woodside Av *BRIX/LBKBY* NN6 ......**26** B4
  NHTNE/MOU NN3 ....**40** D5
Woodside Crs *NHTNE/MOU* NN3 ..**30** D5
Woodside Wk *NHTNW* NN5 ....**50** A1
Woodside Wy *NHTNW* NN5 ....**50** A1
Woodstock Cl *WBORO* NN8 ....**15** G2

Wood St *NHTN* NN1...........................
  RSHD/HF NN10 ....
  WBORO NN8 ....
Woodside Rd *NHTNS* NN4 ....
Woolmonger St *NHTN* NN1 ....
Wooton Ct *NHTNS* NN4 ....
Wootton Hope Dr *NHTNS* NN4 ......
Wootton Brook Cl *NHTNS* NN4 ......
Wootton Hill Farm *NHTNS* NN4 .....
Wootton Hope Dr *NHTNS* NN4 ......
Worcester Cl *NHTNE/MOU* NN3 ....
Wordsworth Rd *WBORO* NN8 ....
Wrekin Cl *NHTNS* NN4 ....
Wrenbury Rd *NHTNW* NN5 ....
Wren Cl *NHTNS* NN4 ....
The Wroe *RSHD/HF* NN10 ....
Wychwood Cl *NHTNW* NN5 ....
Wyckley Cl *IR/RAU/FIN* NN9 ....
Wycliffe Rd *NHTN* NN1 ....
Wye Cl *WBORO* NN8 ....
Wykeham Rd *RSHD/HF* NN10 ....
Wymersley Cl *NHTNS* NN4 ....
Wymington Pk *RSHD/HF* NN10 ......
Wymington Rd *RSHD/HF* NN10 ......
Wysall Rd *NHTNE/MOU* NN3 ....

Yardley Dr *NHTNN/BOU* NN2 ....
Yarrow Cl *RSHD/HF* NN10 ....
Yarwell Sq *NHTNS* NN4 ....
Yelden Cl *RSHD/HF* NN10 ....
Yeldon Ct *WBORO* NN8 ....
Yelvertoft Rd *NHTNN/BOU* NN2 ....
Yeoman Dr *NHTNN/BOU* NN2 ....
Yeoman Meadow *NHTNS* NN4 ....
Yewtree Ct *NHTNE/MOU* NN3 ....
York Av *RNHPTN* NN7 ....
York Cl *IR/RAU/FIN* NN9 ....
Yorke Cl *IR/RAU/FIN* NN9 ....
York Rd *BOZ/IR/WOL* NN29 ....
  NHTN NN1 ....
  RSHD/HF NN10 ....
  WBORO NN8 ....
York Wy *IR/RAU/FIN* NN9 ....

Index - featured places

Abbey Primary School
  NHTNS NN4 ....**61** E4
Abington Business Centre
  NHTN NN1 ....**52** A3
Abington Park Museum
  NHTN NN1 ....**52** A3
Abington Vale Lower School
  NHTNE/MOU NN3 ....**52** B4
Abington Vale Middle School
  NHTNE/MOU NN3 ....**52** C3
Albany House Medical Centre
  WBORO NN8 ....**16** A4
Alfred Street Junior School
  RSHD/HF NN10 ....**33** F2
All Saints CE VA Primary School
  NHTNN/BOU NN2 ....**39** G1
All Saints Primary School
  WBORO NN8 ....**16** B5
Althorp
  RNHPTN NN7 ....**35** G2
Althorp Park
  RNHPTN NN7 ....**35** H3
The Arbours Primary School
  NHTNE/MOU NN3 ....**40** D4
The Avenue Infant School
  WBORO NN8 ....**16** A4
Barry Primary School
  NHTN NN1 ....**52** A3
Bellinge Lower School
  NHTNE/MOU NN3 ....**53** H1
Billing Aquadrome
  Holiday Park
  NHTNE/MOU NN3 ....**53** H2
Billing Brook Special School
  NHTNE/MOU NN3 ....**41** H4
Blackthorn Primary School
  NHTNE/MOU NN3 ....**41** H3
The Bliss Charity School
  RNHPTN NN7 ....**56** C2
Blisworth Primary School
  RNHPTN NN7 ....**71** F3
Boothville School
  NHTNE/MOU NN3 ....**40** C4
Bosworth Independant College
  NHTNN/BOU NN2 ....**51** E2
Boughton Primary School
  NHTNN/BOU NN2 ....**23** F4
Brackmills Business Park
  NHTNS NN4 ....**62** A4
Brackmills Industrial Estate
  NHTNS NN4 ....**62** B3
Brampton Heath Golf Centre
  BRIX/LBKBY NN6 ....**21** G5
The Bramptons
  Primary School
  BRIX/LBKBY NN6 ....**20** C3
Briar Hill Primary School
  NHTNS NN4 ....**60** B2
Brington Primary School
  RNHPTN NN7 ....**34** C4
Brixworth CECV Primary School
  BRIX/LBKBY NN6 ....**4** D5
Brixworth Country Park
  BRIX/LBKBY NN6 ....**13** E2
Brook Medical Centre
  NHTNE/MOU NN3 ....**42** B5
Bugbrooke Primary School
  RNHPTN NN7 ....**57** F4
Bugbrooke RUFC
  RNHPTN NN7 ....**57** G5

Campion School
  RNHPTN NN7 ....**57** G4
Caroline Chisholm School
  NHTNS NN4 ....**68** D2
Castle Primary School
  NHTNN/BOU NN2 ....**51** F2
Castle Theatre & Arts Centre
  WBORO NN8 ....**16** B5
Cedar Road Primary School
  NHTNE/MOU NN3 ....**52** A1
Chichele College
  RSHD/HF NN10 ....**19** F3
Chieftan Business Park
  WBORO NN8 ....**14** C3
Chiltern Primary School
  NHTNS NN4 ....**49** H2
Chowns Mill Business Park
  IR/RAU/FIN NN9 ....**9** H5
Cogenhoe Primary School
  RNHPTN NN7 ....**54** D5
Cogenhoe United FC
  RNHPTN NN7 ....**54** C5
Collingtree CE Primary School
  NHTNS NN4 ....**68** A4
Collingtree Park Golf Club
  NHTNS NN4 ....**67** H3
Collingwood Business Centre
  NHTN NN1 ....**2** A2
The Counties Crematorium
  NHTNS NN4 ....**67** E2
Courtyard by Marriott
  Northampton
  NHTNS NN4 ....**62** B1
Croyland Primary School
  WBORO NN8 ....**29** G1
Danes Camp Leisure Centre
  NHTNS NN4 ....**60** D5
Degra House School
  NHTNN/BOU NN2 ....**39** E5
Delapre Golf Centre
  NHTNS NN4 ....**61** H3
Delapre Medical Centre
  NHTNS NN4 ....**61** H3
Delapre Primary School
  NHTNS NN4 ....**60** D2
Dencora Business Park
  WBORO NN8 ....**14** C4
Denfield Park Junior School
  RSHD/HF NN10 ....**33** F1
Denington Industrial Estate
  WBORO NN8 ....**30** A1
Denton Primary School
  RNHPTN NN7 ....**65** G5
Duston Eldean Primary School
  NHTNW NN5 ....**49** F1
Duston Medical Centre
  NHTNW NN5 ....**49** F3
The Duston School
  NHTNW NN5 ....**49** E2
Earls Barton Junior School
  BRIX/LBKBY NN6 ....**44** A3
Earl Spencer Primary School
  NHTNW NN5 ....**50** C2
Eastfield Primary School
  NHTNE/MOU NN3 ....**40** B5
East Hunsbury
  Primary School
  NHTNS NN4 ....**67** H2
Ecton Brook Primary School
  NHTNE/MOU NN3 ....**42** B5

Ecton Primary School
  BRIX/LBKBY NN6 ....**42** D3
Express Business Park
  RSHD/HF NN10 ....**32** A1
Fairfields School
  NHTNW NN5 ....**51** G1
Ferrers Specialist Arts College
  RSHD/HF NN10 ....**19** G4
Finedon Infant School
  IR/RAU/FIN NN9 ....**7** H1
Finedon Mulso CE Junior School
  IR/RAU/FIN NN9 ....**8** A1
Finedon Road Industrial Estate
  WBORO NN8 ....**6** C5
  WBORO NN8 ....**16** B2
Freemans Endowed
  CE Junior School
  WBORO NN8 ....**15** C5
Friars School
  WBORO NN8 ....**30** A1
Frog Island Brewery
  NHTNW NN5 ....**50** C5
Gayton CE Primary School
  RNHPTN NN7 ....**70** A1
Gibraltar Barracks
  NHTN NN1 ....**2** D1
The Good Shepherd
  Catholic Primary School
  NHTNN/BOU NN2 ....**39** E4
Grammarians FC
  WBORO NN8 ....**6** D5
Grange Park
  Community Centre
  NHTNS NN4 ....**68** C5
Great Doddington
  Primary School
  BOZ/IR/WOL NN29 ....**45** G1
Greenfields School
  NHTNN/BOU NN2 ....**38** D2
Green Oaks Primary School
  NHTNN/BOU NN2 ....**39** E3
Grosvenor Centre
  NHTN NN1 ....**2** E3
Hardingstone Primary School
  NHTNS NN4 ....**68** C1
Hardwick County
  Junior School
  WBORO NN8 ....**15** E4
Hardwick Infant School
  WBORO NN8 ....**15** E4
Harlestone Primary School
  RNHPTN NN7 ....**36** C1
Harpole Primary School
  RNHPTN NN7 ....**48** A4
Hayway Infant School
  RSHD/HF NN10 ....**19** F5
Headlands Primary School
  NHTNE/MOU NN3 ....**40** C5
Henry Chichele Primary School
  RSHD/HF NN10 ....**19** F2
Higham Ferrers Infant School
  IR/RAU/FIN NN9 ....**19** F1
HighField Leisure Centre
  WBORO NN8 ....**16** B4
The Hind Hotel
  WBORO NN8 ....**16** A5
HM Prison
  WBORO NN8 ....**30** A4
Hopping Hill Primary School
  NHTNW NN5 ....**49** G2

Hotel ibis
  NHTNN/BOU NN2 ....**2** C4
Hotel Ibis Wellingborough
  WBORO NN8 ....**29** F3
Hunsbury Hill Country Park
  NHTNS NN4 ....**60** B4
Hunsbury Park Lower School
  NHTNS NN4 ....**60** B3
Huxloe Science College
  IR/RAU/FIN NN9 ....**9** E4
Innkeeper's Lodge
  NHTNE/MOU NN3 ....**41** E1
Innkeeper's Lodge
  (Northampton South)
  NHTNS NN4 ....**68** B3
Irchester Community
  Primary School
  BOZ/IR/WOL NN29 ....**31** G4
Irchester Country Park
  BOZ/IR/WOL NN29 ....**31** E5
Irchester Health Centre
  BOZ/IR/WOL NN29 ....**31** G4
Irthlingborough Infant School
  IR/RAU/FIN NN9 ....**9** E4
Irthlingborough Junior School
  IR/RAU/FIN NN9 ....**9** E4
Isebrook Hospital
  WBORO NN8 ....**30** B1
Ise Valley Industrial Estate
  WBORO NN8 ....**16** D1
JBJ Business Park
  RNHPTN NN7 ....**71** F1
John Dryden House
  (Northamptonshire
  County Council)
  NHTN NN1 ....**62** C1
Kingsfield Business Park
  NHTNW NN5 ....**50** C1
Kings Heath Industrial Estate
  NHTNW NN5 ....**50** B1
Kings Heath Primary School
  NHTNW NN5 ....**38** B5
Kingsley Primary School
  NHTNN/BOU NN2 ....**39** H5
Kings Meadow School
  NHTNS NN4 ....**24** C5
Kings Park Conference
  & Sports Centre
  NHTNN/BOU NN2 ....**39** H1
Kingsthorpe Business Centre
  NHTNN/BOU NN2 ....**38** D5
Kingsthorpe
  Community College
  NHTNN/BOU NN2 ....**39** G2
Kingsthorpe Golf Club
  NHTNN/BOU NN2 ....**39** F5
Kingsthorpe Grove
  Primary School
  NHTNN/BOU NN2 ....**39** E5
Kingsthorpe Shopping Centre
  NHTNN/BOU NN2 ....**39** G2
Kingsthorpe Village
  Primary School
  NHTNN/BOU NN2 ....**38** D4
Kislingbury CC
  RNHPTN NN7 ....**58** C1
Kislingbury VC Primary School
  RNHPTN NN7 ....**58** B1
Leyland Trading Estate
  WBORO NN8 ....**16** D5

Lime Trees Hotel
  NHTNN/BOU NN2 ....
Lings Forum Leisure Centre
  NHTNE/MOU NN3 ....
Lings Lower School
  NHTNE/MOU NN3 ....
Lings Theatre
  NHTNE/MOU NN3 ....
Little Houghton
  CE Primary School
  NHTNE/MOU NN3 ....
Lodge Farm Industrial Estate
  NHTNW NN5 ....
Lumbertubs Primary School
  NHTNE/MOU NN3 ....
Lyncrest Lower School
  NHTNW NN5 ....
Mears Ashby Endowed
  Primary School
  BRIX/LBKBY NN6 ....
Megabowl
  NHTNW NN5 ....
Mereway Community College
  NHTNS NN4 ....
Midland Business Centre
  RSHD/HF NN10 ....
Midland Works Business Centre
  WBORO NN8 ....
Mill Road Industrial Estate
  WBORO NN8 ....
Millway Primary School
  WBORO NN8 ....
Milton Parochial
  Primary School
  RNHPTN NN7 ....
Moat House Hotel
  NHTN NN1 ....
Moulton Business Park
  NHTNE/MOU NN3 ....
Moulton College
  NHTNE/MOU NN3 ....
Moulton Park
  Business Centre
  NHTNE/MOU NN3 ....
Moulton Primary School
  NHTNE/MOU NN3 ....
Moulton School
  NHTNE/MOU NN3 ....
Mount Baths
  NHTN NN1 ....
Mounts Business Centre
  NHTN NN1 ....
Mounts Medical Centre
  NHTN NN1 ....
Nene Valley Retail Park
  NHTNS NN4 ....
Nene White Water Centre
  NHTNS NN4 ....
Newton Road Cemetery
  RSHD/HF NN10 ....
Newton Road Community
  Primary School
  RSHD/HF NN10 ....
Norman-D-Gate
  Industrial Estate
  NHTN NN1 ....
Northampton Academy
  NHTNE/MOU NN3 ....
Northampton Casuals RUFC
  NHTNS NN4 ....

mpton Cathedral
 NN/BOU NN2 ....51 E2
mpton College
 NE/MOU NN3 ....40 D4
mpton
eral Hospital
 N NN1 ....3 H4
mpton Golf Club
 RNHPTN NN7 ....36 C2
mpton High School
 NS NN4 ....61 F5
mpton
mport Railway
 K/LBKBY NN6 ....4 A5
mpton Marriott Hotel
 NS NN4 ....61 H2
mpton Museum
 N NN1
t Gallery
 N NN1 ....2 E4
mpton
paratory School
 N NN1 ....62 D2
mpton Saints RUFC
 nklin Gardens)
 NW NN5 ....50 B4
mpton School for Boys
 N NN1 ....52 A4
mpton School for Girls
 E/MOU NN3 ....40 A3
mptonshire CCC
 N NN1 ....52 A2
mptonshire
 nty Golf Club
 N NN1 ....21 H5
mptonshire
mmar School
 K/LBKBY NN6 ....13 F5
mptonshire Music &
forming Arts Service
 N NN1 ....3 G1
mpton Town FC
 fields Stadium)
 NW NN5 ....49 H5
mpton Visitors Centre
 N NN1 ....2 E4
gate School
 ORO NN2 ....39 E5
ay Infant School
 ORO NN8 ....16 A2
ay Junior School
 ORO NN8 ....16 A3
outs RFC
 N NN1 ....52 B5
en University (WDS)
 ORO NN8 ....30 A3
dys RC Junior School
 ORO NN8 ....29 F1
one Park CC
 K/LBKBY NN6 ....26 A2
one Park Golf Club
 K/LBKBY NN6 ....26 A5
one Park School
 K/LBKBY NN6 ....25 H4
one Primary School
 K/LBKBY NN6 ....25 G3

Park Farm Industrial Estate
 WBORO NN8 ....14 C3
Parkham Industrial Estate
 RSHD/HF NN10 ....18 B5
Park Infant School
 IR/RAU/FIN NN9 ....11 G2
Park Junior School
 WBORO NN8 ....16 A4
Parklands Primary School
 NHTNE/MOU NN3 ....40 A3
Peacock Place
 NHTN NN1 ....2 E3
The Pemberton Leisure
 & Conference Centre
 RSHD/HF NN10 ....32 D2
Penvale Park Medical Centre
 NHTNS NN4 ....61 E5
Pitsford & Brampton Station
 BRIX/LBKBY NN6 ....22 A2
Pitsford Primary School
 BRIX/LBKBY NN6 ....13 F4
Premier Travel Inn
 NHTNE/MOU NN3 ....54 A3
 NHTNS NN4 ....61 F5
 NHTNS NN4 ....62 C2
 RNHPTN NN7 ....48 A5
 WBORO NN8 ....30 B2
Preston Hedges
 Primary School
 NHTNS NN4 ....68 D2
Princess Marina Hospital
 NHTNW NN5 ....49 F4
Prologis Park
 WBORO NN8 ....31 E2
Pytchley Court Health Centre
 NHTNE/MOU NN3 ....4 D5
Quality Hotel Northampton
 NHTNE/MOU NN3 ....40 D5
Queen Eleanor Primary School
 NHTNE/MOU NN3 ....60 D3
Queen Eleanor's Cross
 NHTNS NN4 ....61 E4
Queens Park Industrial Estate
 NHTNN/BOU NN2 ....38 D5
Queensview Medical Centre
 NHTNN/BOU NN2 ....51 E1
Queensway Medical Centre
 WBORO NN8 ....15 E4
Quinton House School
 NHTNW NN5 ....49 F5
Raeburn School
 NHTNN/BOU NN2 ....39 H5
Raunds Medical Centre
 IR/RAU/FIN NN9 ....10 D1
Rectory Farm Primary School
 NHTNE/MOU NN3 ....42 A2
Redwell Infant School
 WBORO NN8 ....15 G2
Redwell Leisure Centre
 WBORO NN8 ....15 G2
Redwell Medical Centre
 WBORO NN8 ....15 G2
The Redwell Medical Centre
 WBORO NN8 ....29 G2
Rillwood Medical Centre
 NHTNE/MOU NN3 ....41 E4

Riverside Business Park
 NHTNE/MOU NN3 ....53 E4
Riverside Retail Park
 RSHD/HF NN10 ....53 E3
Riverside Way Industrial Estate
 NHTN NN1 ....3 J5
Roade Primary School
 RNHPTN NN7 ....73 E4
Roade School Sports College
 RNHPTN NN7 ....72 C5
Rothersthorpe CE
 Primary School
 RNHPTN NN7 ....66 A2
Royal Theatre
 & Derngate Centre
 NHTN NN1 ....2 E4
Rushden Athletic Club
 RSHD/HF NN10 ....33 F2
Rushden Community College
 RSHD/HF NN10 ....19 E5
Rushden & Diamonds FC
 (Nene Park)
 IR/RAU/FIN NN9 ....9 H3
Rushden Hospital
 RSHD/HF NN10 ....33 F4
Rushden Town FC
 RSHD/HF NN10 ....33 G2
Ruskin Infant School
 WBORO NN8 ....29 E1
Ryelands Middle School
 NHTNW NN5 ....49 E2
St Andrews CE Primary School
 NHTNE/MOU NN3 ....42 A5
St. Andrews Hospital
 NHTN NN1 ....52 A4
St Barnabas CE School
 WBORO NN8 ....15 H5
St Gregory's RC Lower School
 NHTNE/MOU NN3 ....40 C3
St James CE Lower School
 NHTNW NN5 ....50 C4
St. James Retail Park
 NHTN NN1 ....2 B6
St Lukes CEVA Primary School
 NHTNW NN5 ....49 G3
St Mary's Catholic
 Lower School
 NHTNW NN5 ....50 A1
St Matthews
 Preparatory School
 NHTN NN1 ....52 A1
St Peters CE Junior School
 IR/RAU/FIN NN9 ....11 G2
St Peters Independent School
 NHTNE/MOU NN3 ....41 G3
Sanders Lodge
 Industrial Estate
 IR/RAU/FIN NN9 ....32 B1
Sileby Rangers FC
 NHTNE/MOU NN3 ....40 C1
Simon de Senlis Lower School
 NHTNS NN4 ....60 D5
Sir Christopher Hatton School
 WBORO NN8 ....16 A3
South End J & I School
 RSHD/HF NN10 ....33 F4

Spinney Brook Medical Centre
 IR/RAU/FIN NN9 ....9 F4
Splash Leisure Pool
 RSHD/HF NN10 ....33 F1
Spring Lane Primary School
 NHTN NN1 ....2 B2
Standens Barn Lower School
 NHTNE/MOU NN3 ....53 F2
Stanwick Primary School
 IR/RAU/FIN NN9 ....10 C5
Stanwick Rovers FC
 IR/RAU/FIN NN9 ....10 B4
Sterling Business Park
 NHTNS NN4 ....62 B4
Stimpson Avenue
 Primary School
 NHTN NN1 ....51 H3
The Summerlee Medical Centre
 IR/RAU/FIN NN9 ....7 H2
Sunnyside Lower School
 NHTNN/BOU NN2 ....39 F1
Super Bowl
 WBORO NN8 ....30 B2
Swan Valley Industrial Park
 NHTNS NN4 ....59 F4
Sywell CE Primary School
 BRIX/LBKBY NN6 ....26 B2
Sywell Country Park
 BRIX/LBKBY NN6 ....27 E5
Tennyson Road Infant School
 RSHD/HF NN10 ....32 D2
Thomas Becket Catholic Upper
 School
 NHTNE/MOU NN3 ....40 B2
Thorplands Lower School
 NHTNE/MOU NN3 ....41 E2
Three Shires Hospital
 NHTN NN1 ....3 K4
Travelodge
 NHTNE/MOU NN3 ....49 H5
 NHTNW NN5 ....59 H1
 WBORO NN8 ....18 B5
Trensham Institute of Further
 Education & Higher Education
 (Wellingborough Campus)
 WBORO NN8 ....16 A4
UGC
 NHTNW NN5 ....49 H5
Unity College
 NHTNN/BOU NN2 ....51 F1
The University of Northampton
 (Avenue Campus)
 NHTNS NN4 ....51 F1
The University of Northampton
 (Park Campus)
 NHTNN/BOU NN2 ....39 G2
Vernon Terrace Lower School
 NHTN NN1 ....3 J3
Victoria Business Park
 NHTNW NN5 ....2 A3
Victoria Infant School
 WBORO NN8 ....16 B3
Victoria Junior School
 WBORO NN8 ....16 B4
Warwick Primary School
 WBORO NN8 ....29 G3

Weavers School
 WBORO NN8 ....15 F5
Weedon Road Industrial Estate
 NHTNW NN5 ....50 B4
Wellingborough Golf Club
 IR/RAU/FIN NN9 ....6 A4
Wellingborough
 Heritage Centre
 WBORO NN8 ....16 A5
Wellingborough Junior School
 WBORO NN8 ....30 B1
Wellingborough Medical Centre
 WBORO NN8 ....16 A3
Wellingborough
 Preparatory School
 WBORO NN8 ....30 B1
Wellingborough RFC
 BOZ/IR/WOL NN29 ....45 E1
Wellingborough
 Swimming Baths
 WBORO NN8 ....29 H1
Wellingborough Town CC
 WBORO NN8 ....15 G3
Wellingborough Town FC
 WBORO NN8 ....30 B1
Welsh House
 NHTN NN1 ....2 D5
Weston Favell CE
 Primary School
 NHTNE/MOU NN3 ....52 D1
Weston Favell School
 NHTNE/MOU NN3 ....40 D5
Weston Favell
 Shopping Centre
 NHTNE/MOU NN3 ....41 F5
Whitefriars J & I School
 RSHD/HF NN10 ....32 D3
Whitehills Primary School
 NHTNN/BOU NN2 ....38 C1
White House Industrial Estate
 BRIX/LBKBY NN6 ....43 H1
Willby CE Primary School
 WBORO NN8 ....28 D3
Windmill Primary School
 NHTN NN1 ....11 E1
Wollaston Community
 Primary School
 BOZ/IR/WOL NN29 ....46 D3
Wollaston School
 BOZ/IR/WOL NN29 ....47 E3
Woodland View
 Primary School
 NHTNS NN4 ....68 C5
Woodvale Primary School
 NHTNE/MOU NN3 ....41 G2
Wootton Medical Centre
 NHTNS NN4 ....68 C2
Wootton Primary School
 NHTNS NN4 ....68 C2
Wrenn School
 WBORO NN8 ....30 B1

Acknowledgements

Post Office is a registered trademark of Post Office Ltd. in the UK and other countries.

ols address data provided by Education Direct.

l station information supplied by Johnsons

way street data provided by © Tele Atlas N.V. Tele Atlas

en centre information provided by

en Centre Association  Britains best garden centres

ale Garden Centres

statement on the front cover of this atlas is sourced, selected and quoted
a reader comment and feedback form received in 2004